THE INTERTEXTUALITY OF FATE

JOHN HANNAY

THE INTERTEXTUALITY
OF FATE

A STUDY OF MARGARET DRABBLE

A LITERARY FRONTIERS EDITION, NO. 28
UNIVERSITY OF MISSOURI PRESS
COLUMBIA, 1986

Library of Congress Cataloging-in-Publication Data

Hannay, John.
    The intertextuality of fate.
    Includes bibliographical references.
    1. Drabble, Margaret, 1939–   Criticism and
interpretation.   2. Fate and fatalism in literature.
I. Title.
PR6054.R25Z69   1986   823'.912   85–20957
ISBN 0-8262-0499-6 (alk. paper)

∞^{TM} This paper meets the minimum requirements of
the American National Standard for Permanence of Paper
for Printed Library Materials, Z39.48, 1984.

Cover photograph by Mark Gerson

I dedicate this book to my wife,
Jayme,
to whom I owe more than words can express.

CONTENTS

I. Introduction, 1

II. The Tragic Romance: *The Waterfall*, 18

III. The Return to Origin: *The Needle's Eye*, 48

IV. The Providential Model: *The Ice Age*, 77

V. Conclusion, 100

Selected Works by Margaret Drabble, 112

I. Introduction

Margaret Drabble receives much praise, and condemnation, for writing more like George Eliot or Arnold Bennett than James Joyce. One example of her traditionalism can be seen in her almost quaint belief that the word *fate* will carry conviction for the modern reader. But she also plays with this word in a self-reflexive manner that reorients its traditional meanings and generates new levels of irony regarding the self-awareness of characters. While several critics have commented on the theme of fate in Drabble's works, they have missed her textual irony and so have failed to comprehend a major aspect of her originality.

The word *fate* may have lost its currency as metaphysical doctrine, but it still crops up frequently in colloquial uses. We find the phrases "as fate would have it" or "a fateful meeting" ready at hand to define patterns that appear comprehensible, or at least discernible, to us. They fit well-known stories to present circumstances. We would not use such phrases to describe utterly meaningless combinations of events, nor to describe perfectly ordinary ones. Rather, we use them to define unexpected events that in retrospect seem appropriate in ways that go beyond mere chance. Life suddenly becomes like a narrative, whose intentionality guides throughout.

One's fate is decreed at birth, like a story whose point inheres from the very beginning but is not fully apparent until the end. The story may appear at times to contradict the formal logic of its plot, just as a character may struggle against fate, but the end reveals an inevitability governing the whole. The impression of inevitability depends on the similarity of the narrative pattern of events to many other stories in terms of plot, character, theme, or images. We "know what comes next" because we recall analogous stories and so discern the proleptic logic of the one we are reading.

Freud believed uncanny experiences reawakened childhood memories, and we might say analogously that fateful moments reawaken memories of familiar stories. As structuralists are quick to point out, these associations derive from the elemental patterns that stories share with one another. Stories of childhood tragedies surfacing late in life, star-crossed lovers, heroic confrontations that end with hollow victories, fortune always coming to one brother and not the other: not only our literary heritage but also our general culture abounds with such paradigmatic plots. Events we term fated seem to emerge from and to conform to this common culture, as if they had been foreordained. The term *intertextuality* describes this sense of life repeating a previously heard story, of life predestined by the patterns that have shaped our consciousness.

The intertext of a given story is the set of plots, characters, images, generic codes, and literary conventions it calls to mind for a given reader. The term *intertext* allows one to speak of these elements as a totality, creating a general sense of a work of art reflecting a tradition, without limiting that sense to individual elements. The intertext is not simply another text to which a work alludes directly or indirectly. Multiple texts or verbal messages are present in any given text through shared elements, and *intertext* refers to these shared aspects rather than simply to the texts themselves. The shared elements are what Northrop Frye calls a "symbol," "any unit of any literary structure that can be isolated for critical attention," and the intertext is the set of what Frye defines as "archetypes," "symbols which connect one poem with another and thereby help to unify and integrate our literary experience."[1]

1. Northrop Frye, *Anatomy of Criticism: Four Essays*, 1957 (rpt. New York: Atheneum, 1970). See p. 71 for discussion of symbols and p. 91 for discussion of archetypes.

While a narrative generally evokes several models, one will tend to dominate and to unify the whole. Thus we may, for the purpose of our discussion, refer to a particular model or to a generic plot and all its associated imagery and conventions as "the intertext" for a given story, realizing, of course, that this narrows and simplifies the work's total intertext. An intertext may be explicitly alluded to in the story, or it may be a general association in the reader's mind. Joyce's *Ulysses* refers in its title to a specific model for its homecoming pattern, but it also invokes this intertext indirectly through various comments by the narrator and by the characters. The intertext may also derive from cultural norms, popular media, common sayings, and linguistic conventions relating to concepts such as fate, though in my study I concentrate on literary norms and conventions.

Clearly the concept of intertextuality presumes a reader's general literacy and competency in interpreting texts, but specific aspects of the intertext will vary, as do all critical interpretations, with each reader's particular background. We need not argue that an author has a specific work in mind that establishes the intertext. Certainly an allusion in the text or a reference in interviews, letters, or journals may provide helpful clues. But allusions are only beginning points for seeking common elements between texts. A reader constructs an intertext, whether or not such specific references are available, out of the codes and the conventions governing the form, genre, and style of a given text.

Since literary works incorporate these conventions self-consciously, we must go beyond simply identifying them and decide how they contribute to the aesthetic ends of the signifying system. Michael Riffaterre, in defending his theory of intertextuality against the charge of reductionism, maintains he seeks not just the *matrix* or *hypogram* (his terms for the intertext) that a given work of art presupposes but also its many variants.[2] New relationships continually evolve between the text and the intertext as they play off against one another. Jonathan Culler describes the intertext as allowing a "dialectical opposition which the text presents to result in a synthesis at a higher level where the grounds of intelligibility are different."[3] We read the literary work and construct in our minds a sense of the intertextual models governing its structure and its language. From this initial sense, we test and refine our model, finding ever-changing relationships and combinations in the dialectical opposition between the text and the intertext. From this continual interplay, we may infer a third level at which the text, in commenting on the intertext, comments on how literature relates to reality through conventions. Culler illustrates this dialectic in a later work while discussing the intertextual theories and methods of Julia Kristeva and Harold Bloom, both of whom insist on identifying "pretexts" or intertexts with which the work wrestles.[4] These critics find in the opposition between a text and the discursive space of language and narrative structure that surrounds it a commentary on the tradition within which it generates its meaning.

Realistic fiction often creates its intertextual dialectic by displacing plots from earlier genres, such as the romance tradition or moral parables, into the realm of the ordinary. Hardy's *Life's Little Ironies* takes fablelike stories and adds twists of fate that create a sense of realism and inevitability out of ironic deflation. In one story, "An Imaginative Woman," a young woman keeps the picture of a

2. Michael Riffaterre, *Semiotics of Poetry* (Bloomington: Indiana University Press, 1978), p. 12.

3. Jonathan Culler, *Structuralist Poetics: Structuralism, Linguistics and the Study of Literature* (London: Routledge and Kegan Paul, 1975), p. 151.

4. Culler, *The Pursuit of Signs: Semiotics, Literature, Deconstruction* (Ithaca: Cornell University Press, 1981), pp. 105–111.

melancholy, romantic poet she longed to meet. Despite her contrivances, she never meets him, and this causes her some bitterness. The picture ironically looks like her child, which makes her husband insanely jealous. Though she starts to tell him the truth, she dies before she can finish, making him all the more suspicious. The woman's machinations transform a common tale of romantic passion, doomed from the start as we can quickly tell from the description of the recluse poet, into ridiculous, but painful, irony. Her repeatedly thwarted plans make her appear not only foolish, which she is, but also unfaithful, which she is not. The mistaken identity and abortive deathbed confession further confirm the tragic romance as an intertext, parodying through ironic realism the motif of lovers united in death despite the opposition of society.

These short stories of Hardy comment on their intertexts by implying that reality is harsher and more degrading than they allow. Drabble adapts their dialectic in *The Millstone* and makes Hardy's *Life's Little Ironies* itself stand for an intertext. Rosamund's friend Lydia refuses to write in her novel about her accident (being hit by a bus and thus spontaneously achieving the abortion she had been unsuccessfully seeking) saying, "It's so unconvincing. Far too unrealistic for my kind of novel. It sounds like something out of Hardy's *Life's Little Ironies*." She cites the Hardy text in order to acknowledge, but then reject, the class of stories for which her accident would be suitable, stories with strongly ironic, sudden twists of fate. We see here how much an intertext depends on the reader's interpretive stance: Lydia feels her accident would seem contrived if used in her "realistic" fiction. But Lydia's rejection is dialectically countered in the passage as a whole, for Lydia's denial of Hardy's twists of fate is spoken in the context of an accident that would fit his conventions and that really did happen. Moreover, Rosamund, clearly Drabble's spokesperson, counters with, "'I've always thought *Life's Little Ironies* had rather a profound attitude to life.'"[5]

Frequently Drabble's novels repeat this pattern, first denying conventions in the name of realism and then reaffirming them by suggesting that "realism" should be broadened to include such conventions. The denial disarms criticism by assuring the reader that the narrative will not force a belief in extraordinary happenstance. All will go according to familiar laws of reality. The reversal of this denial usually takes the form of "truth stranger than fiction." This phrase succinctly describes a two-stage logic that says, first, "realistic" fiction does not contain strange or highly significant coincidences, the stuff of melodrama; and, second, "truth" in real life does contain such amazing coincidences. "Fate" often implies the possibility of a "truth stranger than fiction," a truth whose design and implications seem more symbolic than most "realistic" fiction would permit. Drabble pushes dialectically at the boundaries of realistic novels so as to reorient traditional paradigms of fate and to generate new levels of philosophic and poetic meanings. Susan Stewart has described ways that fictional play with conventions of truth leads to boundary problems, a realism more real than "real life" because touching more directly on myth.[6]

My method will be to look for the simple paradigmatic structures of fate that Drabble's "realistic" surface plays against, and frequently denies, in the name of verisimilitude. Then I will show that her text reasserts these intertextual structures with a plot that conforms, however indirectly, to mythical patterns of fate. Drabble does give fate its

5. Margaret Drabble, *The Millstone* (London: Weidenfeld and Nicolson, 1965), p. 75. Also published as *Thank You All Very Much* (New York: Signet, 1969).

6. Susan Stewart, *Nonsense: Aspects of Intertextuality in Folklore and Literature* (Baltimore: Johns Hopkins University Press, 1980), pp. 19–20.

due, but her indirection warns us not to be too literal in analyzing her thought and narrative methods. Of her nine novels, I have chosen three that vary widely in their techniques for incorporating their intertexts. *The Waterfall* makes the dialectic part of the interplay between two modes of narration; *The Needle's Eye* more traditionally works through structures of plot and imagery; and *The Ice Age* experiments with multiple simultaneous scenes. All these works rely heavily on allusions to literary works and on traditions to guide the reader in identifying their intertexts.

While Drabble resists excessively literary fiction, maintaining that she wants to tell stories based on real life, she acknowledges that real life often structures itself according to patterns familiar from literary tradition. Drabble often has the characters themselves become conscious of their fate in intertextual terms that implicitly claim the models are real, and not just literary convention. Of course, as we saw above with *The Millstone*, the denial of convention in the name of realism is itself a convention and as such has multiple intertexts associated with it. One never escapes entirely from the cultural encodings that shape our language; they are our fate. But we may manipulate the codes for various effects, with varying degrees of self-awareness. If our resistance to one model inevitably creates conformity to another, still such conformity may bring a more complete, even more profound viewpoint.

So far we have been assuming that fate calls attention to a narrative's intertext by suggesting the quality of closure operating in the plot. C. C. Barfoot, in a discussion of fate as being the "plottedness" of life, contrasts it with a sense of open-endedness:

> In so far as the novel requires formal economy, it demands preparation and will tend to stress the provenance and power of fate; in so far as it is required to be true to the natural life that surrounds its readers, it should not seem over-prepared

and its curtailed relations must give a persuasive illusion of infinitude.[7]

This opposition of fatedness and verisimilitude makes static the dynamic opposition of text and intertext; it suggests that the intertext creates a sense of inevitability in a plot, against which strains an apparently contingent clutter of realistic details and the freedom of the characters' wills.

Nabokov fulminates against this idea of a dividing line between the logic of fate and the caprice of reality:

> What even the greatest playwrights have never realized is that chance is not always stumbling and that the tragedies of real life are based on the beauty and horror of chance—not merely on its ridiculousness. And it is this secret rhythm of chance that one would like to see pulsating in the veins of the tragic muse. . . . It would be absurd to suggest that accident and chance may be left to play havoc with life on the stage. But it is not absurd to say that a writer of genius may discover exactly the right harmony of such accidental occurrences, and that this harmony, without suggesting anything like the iron laws of tragic fatality, will express certain definite combinations that occur in life.[8]

Fate ambiguously includes necessity and chance. Although Greek tragedians required a notion of fate that adhered to strict logical rules, the Greeks also called their goddesses of fate "*moirae*," meaning "portion" or "lot," as in "drawn by lot." In this respect, they personified Fate's dual nature as being so compelling as to be unalterable, yet determined by laws so mysterious as to seem like chance.

Drabble, too, understands this duality and, like Hardy before her, relies on coincidence and on chance to create her sense of fate. Her novels do not present a merely static

---

7. C. C. Barfoot, *The Thread of Connection: Aspects of Fate in the Novels of Jane Austen and Others* (Amsterdam: Rodopi, 1982), p. 152.

8. Vladimir Nabokov, "The Tragedy of Tragedy: When Will Playwrights Leave Fate to Chance?," *Harper's* (October 1984): 85.

opposition between fateful intertexts and realistic detail; rather, they present a true dialectic whereby the whims of destiny gradually take on structure and form. The climactic scenes in the three novels whose intertexts I analyze (the car accident in *The Waterfall*, the chase after Christopher in *The Needle's Eye*, and Anthony's imprisonment in Walacia in *The Ice Age*) all introduce unexpected, yet somehow predestined, developments in character through chance occurrences. They fulfill the intertext at the moment they very nearly elude it.

Fate labels and by that labeling equates a logic of mysterious causality or chance with cultural and literary norms. Lydia objects to including her bus accident because it depended on chance to bring good fortune and to wrap things up neatly. She calls this model mechanical, but ironically her expectations have derived from a much more mechanically deterministic model: the naturalistic novel's assumption that chance invariably causes misfortune. Drabble's ironic presentation of Lydia's critique makes life's little ironies all the more compelling. Drabble challenges the reader to find an intertext that will create a harmony out of coincidence and accidental occurrences yet not constrict them to lifeless mechanism.

I concentrate on what I consider to be the principle intertextual paradigm of fate in each of the three novels I discuss (among the many possible dimensions of their intertexts). While I am guided by the terms the novels set for themselves, my description of the intertext remains a matter of critical explication, not a study of sources and of allusions. While the conventional patterns of fate underlying Drabble's novels do not fit simply into a small number of categories, neither are they totally amorphous. Drabble tends to repeat a few general paradigms associated with the word *fate*.

My categories form a sequence that suggests one major

line of development in Drabble's career to date. I begin with the model of tragic romance—in which a passionate, illicit love fatally draws two characters together in a union that seems destined to end in death—because much of her earlier fiction centers on the choice of love as a solution to characters' existential dilemmas. Drabble's first four novels (*A Summer Bird-Cage*, *The Garrick Year*, *The Millstone*, and *Jerusalem the Golden*) all treat young women tempted into extramarital or adulterous affairs, yet withholding physically and emotionally from an erotic relationship and generally finding little satisfaction in sex. Ellen Rose sees Clara Maugham's problem, in *Jerusalem the Golden*, as one of autonomy rather than of sex and gender,[9] but Clara does find her sexual initiation disillusioning. The pleasure she derives from her lover, Gabriel Denham, originates more in her sense of illicit adventure than in any physical desire she feels.

Jane Gray, in Drabble's fifth novel, *The Waterfall*, starts out sexually stymied, but she learns the powerful attraction of love from James Otford, her cousin's husband. She experiences a deeply satisfying orgasm that marks the culmination of her sexual initiation as well as marks the high point of Drabble's preoccupation with sex. Jane's love for James remains illicit and comes near to causing their deaths. In subsequent novels, Drabble appears to have passed on to other concerns, and her heroines all take it pretty much as a matter of course that sex can be pleasurable when the right lover comes along. None of her later heroines fears sex or has significant conflicts about it.

The power of sexual attraction has so often been the theme of literature that one cannot write about it without invoking one of several familiar models: love as salvation, love as curse, love as both salvation and curse, love as disil-

9. Ellen Rose, *The Novels of Margaret Drabble* (Totowa, N.J.: Barnes & Noble, 1980), p. 49.

lusionment, and so on. As Tony Tanner describes, adultery dominates narratives of romance, for it epitomizes the conflict of love with the rules controlling society.[10] The subject of *The Waterfall* is sexual love, not society, family, or even compassion. It presents the search for existential honesty and the language of self solely in terms of romance, rejecting the claims of children. "Fate" appears more often (and it appears quite often) in this novel in relation to her initiation into love than anything else. Jane worries about her effect on her children and the fate they will inherit from her, but her concern for them remains peripheral to the main plot.

Following *The Waterfall*, Drabble turns her attention much more to the responsibilities of motherhood as providing the terms and structures by which she defines fate. Although continuing to write plots based on adultery, she emphasizes the claims of the family. In *The Waterfall*, Jane's husband, Malcolm, does make an isolated attempt to exert a claim on the children, but he steps back quickly and, it seems, gratuitously. He fits the role of cuckolded and outraged husband from romance stories much more than a model of family concerns. But Christopher Vasiliou, Rose's husband in *The Needle's Eye*, is quite a different case. His reappearance and his attempts to reclaim their three children centrally govern the plot and lead to the climactic scene in Rose's childhood home. Christopher's marriage to Rose has something of the flavor of Malcolm's to Jane and likewise leads to separation because of physical abuse as

10. Tony Tanner, *Adultery in the Novel: Contract and Transgression* (Baltimore: John Hopkins University Press, 1979), pp. 11–18; Hannay, Interview of Drabble, 21 and 25 June 1985: "In a way, there's an element of *Madame Bovary*, and the adultress relationship, that is the only one dignified enough for fiction. Of course, *Madame Bovary* is a travesty of it, as indeed is *The Waterfall*. Nevertheless, I feel there is a very deeply embedded notion that the forbidden passion is the furious passion. Also that it should be fatal. It is adulterous, and you are meant to die at the end of it— Romeo and Juliet. You are meant to be separated by circumstances, then violently, against your will, joined—like Tristan and Isolde, I suppose."

well as sexual conflict. But Christopher pursues Rose, and she finally accepts him back, resigning herself to the fatality that led her to marry him in the first place.

Rose's children, especially Konstantin, display much more personality and claim more of the reader's sympathy than any of the children in Drabble's earlier novels. We hardly get to know anything about Emma Evans's or Jane Gray's children, and though Rosamund Stacey's baby quickly gains our interest and sympathy, she remains more a symbol of Rosamund's maturation rather than a member of a family. Each of these mothers experiences a crisis of responsibility, indicating that Drabble's deepest moral principles lie with family. But this theme finds its fullest expression in Rose Vasiliou's motherhood, which comes alive in such rich and convincing detail. Furthermore, a narrative structure based on a return to origin—in which a character returns home and rediscovers his or her destiny in determining family influences—allows a broader scope and a deeper examination of the theme of motherhood. In acknowledging her inherited family ties as determinative of her search for self, Rose accepts the necessity for remarrying Christopher.

Drabble moves beyond, though she never abandons, the symbolism of the family for defining fate as universal design. In *The Realms of Gold*, Frances Wingate's children never seem very real, and her commitment to her family appears to demand little self-sacrifice and to yield little self-knowledge. Frances combines comic romance with a return to origin by finding in Karel the solution to both her love and her family inheritance. More important, Frances's anthropological training leads her to become preoccupied with her ancestral depression on a more general, sociological level than Rose's concerns about her parents.

Drabble continues to move beyond the individual in *The Ice Age*, as its title, epigraphs, and allusions to Providence and contemporary problems of English society attest. The adulterous affair between Anthony and Alison leads to no permanent or even compelling solutions, and Anthony's return to his origin is briefly sketched. The children are significant, to be sure, but more symbolic than Rose's children. Molly, Alison's second child, born with cerebral palsy, serves as a touchstone of the compassion and the humanity of the other characters (her older sister, her mother, and Anthony) and as a measure of the justice of Providence. Jane, while an interesting teenager in her own right, figures as symbol of cultural and spiritual imprisonment. The structure of the controlling Providential model—in which the guilt of a protagonist is linked with the ills of society, which are healed only when that guilt is expiated according to divine justice—focuses on the fate of England and Anthony's attempt to "justify the ways of God to man."

Drabble continues her sociological perspective in *The Middle Ground* and expects her next novel will extend this journalistic vein.[11] In *The Middle Ground*, she again presents the possibilities of the tragic romance in the form of adulterous love and a return to origin in Kate's return to Bromley. But neither model adequately defines the plot, which pushes toward the Providential model as it emerges from the book's presentation of London. Evidently, the book failed to satisfy Drabble because of its heroine's irresolution[12] and, we might say, its lack of a model of fate to give it structure.

11. Hannay, Interview of Drabble: "I am very interested in the documentary novel, in the variety of things happening and our partial apprehension of them. It is very difficult to find a form, and I didn't feel like I'd succeeded in *The Middle Ground* in finding a form to represent the simultaneity of goings-on. And I think that's what I'm struggling with at the moment, trying to portray contemporary Britain—social attitudes, the way people behave, the way they dress or think—through a variety of viewpoints. The last thing it is is recollection in tranquility—it is not that at all. I suppose there is a difference between journalism and the longer perspective of fiction. I'm not really interested in the longer perspective at the moment; I'm interested in just working out what is happening now."

12. In addition to the comments cited in the previous note, Drabble also said, "Kate, in *The Middle Ground*, has made herself a little kind of fairy-

Drabble critics agree that her novels so far have developed from narrowly restricted characters and concerns to a wider cast of characters and a broader range of themes. As Pamela Bromberg puts it, "If we look at the evolution of narrative form in Drabble's corpus we can see a clear development away from the bildungsroman toward a structure that is communal and process-oriented rather than individual and finite."[13] Joanne Creighton and Bonnie Amodio, finding the more narrowly conceived, psychological studies of the earlier novels more aesthetically accomplished, feel that Drabble has not found the right voice for the broader-based social realism she attempts in her later novels. Other critics, such as Bromberg and Michael Harper, applaud the broadening perspective, finding the earlier one limits her characters.[14] Much of the debate centers on the female protagonists of the later novels, particularly Frances Wingate and Kate Armstrong, who seem so much less conflicted (Creighton would say "double-voiced") than the earlier female protagonists. The burden of fate has lightened for these heroines, though not for other characters in these novels, particularly Janet Bird, Stephen Ollerenshaw, Alison Murray, Anthony Keating, and Peter Fletcher.

Drabble seeks in her later novels, and will undoubtedly continue to seek, a broader perspective that places less emphasis on individual characters than on the destiny of her

tale cottage, really. She's made herself a cozy little cottage where she sits, in her kind of rather romantic little fairy-story house, where everybody's happy and jolly. There is a bit of *Little Women* in it—everyone is busy and happy and being nice to each other. Part of her wants to break up and go to Baghdad. But another part of her knows she can't go yet."

13. Pamela Bromberg, "Narrative in Margaret Drabble's *The Middle Ground*: Relativity versus Teleology," *Contemporary Literature* 24, 4 (1983): 465.

14. Joanne V. Creighton, *Margaret Drabble* (New York: Methuen, 1985), pp. 16, 111; Bonnie Ann Solowich Amodio, "The Novels of Margaret Drabble," Ph.D. Diss. (University of Michigan, 1980), pp. 194–98, 203–213; Michael F. Harper, "Margaret Drabble and the Resurrection of the English Novel," *Contemporary Literature* 23, 2 (1982): 167–68.

society. The conflicts do not disappear, and her attitude toward fate remains the acceptance of, not rebellion against, inherent limits. But the narrative structures consist more of a dialogue between the individual and a wider community than between internal aspects of the self. Mary Moran correctly places the emphasis in her study of Drabble's novels on "the universal, timeless issues" lying behind the contemporary problems of individuals, particularly fate, nature, and the family.[15] I would also agree with Moran that these "structures" of community, though more generalized in Drabble's later works, are no less profoundly conceived.

But to see the depth of Drabble's vision, one must examine the "double-voice" that Creighton finds expressive of the conflict within a character, even if this is not as intensely individualistic in the later novels as it is in the earlier novels. Moran starts with the thesis that Drabble envisions a bleak fate, only briefly interrupted by moments of grace in which the characters, through family, nature, imagination, or good fortune, find moments of solace to help them continue. But, as I have argued elsewhere,[16] Moran, despite her thesis, overemphasizes Drabble's optimism. At one point, after discussing Stephen Ollerenshaw's suicide and Frances's rationalization about his "admirable determination" in facing his own nature, Moran writes, "Thus, Drabble finds nothing lamentable about self-destructive behavior if it follows from one's true nature."[17] Drabble's ache with the pain of such depressive characters as Stephen, and Frances's comment shows her limited vision, not Drabble's. If we do not have a sense of irony condemning Frances here, we gloss over the trenchant paradox of accepting

15. Mary Hurley Moran, *Margaret Drabble: Existing Within Structures,* Crosscurrents Series (Carbondale: Southern Illinois University Press, 1983), pp. 16–17.
16. Hannay, "Margaret Drabble: The Paradox of Grace," *Contemporary Literature* 26, 2 (1985): 240–42.
17. Moran, *Margaret Drabble,* p. 39.

fate, that tragedy remains tragedy even while leading to regeneration in another sphere. More generally, Moran is so intent on showing the "structures" of family, nature, vision, and imagination as bringing unqualified renewal and hope that she neglects the darker aspects to fate her thesis admits.

Valerie Myer, in an amorphous but cogent study, defines the enduring conflict in Drabble's works with steadier insight. She finds no happy perspective from which suicidal and depressive guilt can be rationalized, and she condemns the puritanism leading to such guilt. Myer does not see Drabble's characters as following their true nature to an unqualified healthy adjustment, as Moran asserts,[18] but rather she acknowledges the painful compromises they are forced to make due to their Puritan backgrounds.[19]

By investigating the intertextuality of fate, we can suggest the dialectical opposition by which Drabble defines self-knowledge and grace. Her characters achieve wisdom, to greater or lesser degrees, by recognizing the intertext of their fate and, in different ways, by accommodating its demands. One might think this wisdom would bring hope that grace would relieve or lighten the burden of fate. But for Drabble, wisdom alone cannot alter one's destiny. In fact, awareness of fate and attempts to avoid it often ironically become the means for its fulfillment. Drabble's text imitates this irony by reflecting on the plot conventions that emerge from the characters' struggles with their fates. In both the text and the characters' imagined lives, resistance to a model ironically ends by affirming its universality. Drabble's intertextual play suggests that the terms for articulating conflict are embedded ineradicably in the cultural codes and conventions that shape one's consciousness.

Jane Gray, in *The Waterfall*, finds the intertext of tragic ro-

18. Ibid., p. 14.
19. Valerie Grosvenor Myer, *Margaret Drabble: Puritanism and Permissiveness* (New York: Barnes and Noble, 1974), pp. 17–26, 110–111.

mance plaguing her even at the end, where she partly accepts and partly resents paying the price for her sexual liberation. She cannot recast the story of her life wholly in the form of tragic romance, but neither can she reject this model. Her ambivalence becomes her fate, leaving her dissatisfied, though wiser. Rose Vasiliou, in *The Needle's Eye*, claims at most a heroism, at worst a resignation, in accepting back her husband, but she knows more about why she must do it as a result of her visit home. Though her consciousness of the intertext of a return to origin contributed to her acceptance and makes her more admirable because more self-aware, it is not what accounts for the moments of grace that dignify her simplicity and ennoble her suffering. Anthony Keating, in *The Ice Age*, justifies the ways of God to man, we are told, but he cannot communicate his vision from his prison in Wallacia, and we suspect he will find it disappears if he is freed and returns to England. The Providential model remains incomplete, depending on our judgment of Anthony's ambiguous and possibly ironic revelation. All these characters come to a greater understanding of their fate by recognizing and by identifying the intertext controlling their consciousness. But consciousness alone, in Drabble's world, cannot bring freedom from the determinants of personality.

II. The Tragic Romance: The Waterfall

The socially disruptive force of a fatal, illicit passion can generate many different narrative structures and conventions, but that passion almost always finds its fulfillment in death or banishment. Tragic romances, we might say, form a sub-genre within the larger genre of romance, which usually refers to stories that end with a happy union of lovers following various misadventures and misunderstandings. The story of Lancelot and Guinevere, among many others, shows how elements of tragic romance can subsist within the context of romance. As Gillian Beer asserts, *romance* is an endlessly expansive term: "The rhythms of the interwoven stories in the typical romance construction correspond to the way we interpret our own experience as multiple, endlessly interpenetrating stories, rather than simply as a procession of banal happenings." Northrop Frye has also shown the capacity of romance to assimilate stories, including comedy as well as tragedy.[1] If we choose one story as our model, we are likely to touch on many others indirectly.

The story *Tristan and Isolde* hypostatizes fate in a love potion that transforms the loyal liege and nephew, Tristan, into an adulterous betrayer of his lord and uncle, King Mark. Tristan and Isolde, in almost all versions of the story, express their love in song and poetry, which sometimes leads to an apotheosis of the god of love in art. Often this love lyric finds its setting outside of society, for within King Mark's court the lovers are hounded by their enemies and by the laws they have broken. There can be no reconciliation, for the force of their love, embodied in the fateful

1. Gillian Beer, *The Romance* (London: Methuen, 1970), p. 9; Northrop Frye, *The Secular Scripture: A Study of the Structure of Romance* (Cambridge: Harvard University Press, 1976), p. 15.

power of the love potion, derives from its opposition to the limits of society. Their only hope is to be exalted and united in death, a fate that has inspired artists from Gottfried von Strassburg to Wagner and Mann.

Realistic fiction plays off against the conventions of tragic romance in the name of making "fate" a matter more of character than of magic. The realistic novel emphasizes the known, social world rather than the hidden dreams of that world exposed by romance.[2] Mann, in "Tristan," substitutes for a fatal potion and for Cave of Love Frau Kloeterjahn's tuberculosis in a sanatorium. The romance in that story verges on the dream the medieval legend embodied but parodies the exultation of love in death by having Frau Kloeterjahn die from singing the *liebestod* theme from Wagner's *Tristan*. The lovers in this story serve the great theme of art, but they also seem more debased by their passions than they are exalted. *Anna Karenina* and *Madame Bovary* end with similar ironic fates, in which delusive dreams lead to utter disillusionment and grotesque death.

Margaret Drabble has invoked the tragic romance quite often, and with elaborate explicitness. Most of her lovers indulge adulterous or extramarital passions: Louise and John in *A Summer Bird-Cage*, Emma and Wyndham in *The Garrick Year*, Rosamund and George in *The Millstone*, Clara and Gabriel in *Jerusalem the Golden*, Jane and James in *The Waterfall*, Frances and Karel in *The Realms of Gold*, Anthony and Alison in *The Ice Age*, and Kate and Ted in *The Middle Ground*, not to mention the lovers in "Crossing the Alps" and "Faithful Lovers." *Jerusalem the Golden*, written just before *The Waterfall*, has particularly strong elements of the tragic romance: Clara Maugham's dazzled, fateful first encounters with Clelia Denham and her lover, Gabriel Denham; her overwhelming sense of fate drawing her into a dangerous liaison with him; and her sense of retribution

2. Beer, *Romance*, p. 12.

for their passion when her mother develops cancer during their trip to Paris. While Drabble shies away from having her protagonists die for love, she does portray this passion as unstable, dangerous, and often destructive. Only in *The Realms of Gold* does love end in marriage rather than in dissolution or in social ostracism.

The Waterfall employs the tragic romance over and over again, almost excessively. Drabble describes the story as "this very forceful image of romantic, almost thirteenth-century love."[3] The lovers seem cloistered from society not only by their almost exclusive confinement to one house but also by the turgid narrative style that works to make their encounters seem more self-involved. Drabble counters the sections imitating the tragic romance with sections mocking its conventions through parody and self-referentiality. The contrast in narrative styles presents an exceptionally clear example of the dialectical opposition possible between the tragic romance model and the "realistic" narrative. Through this contrast, Drabble explores in complex ways the possibilities of a synthesis of these modes, as the first-person narrator gains greater consciousness of the nature and the consequences of her romance fantasy.

While the love between Jane Gray and her cousin's husband, James Otford, does not end in death, Drabble plays with that possibility as a climactic convergence of chance and the judgment of fate. Jane, one of the few artists in Drabble's works, writes poetry to express the destructive side of passion, and, supposedly, she also writes the narrative of *The Waterfall* to express its transcendence. She frequently appeals to fate, and her fatalism merges with her acceptance of the tragic romance. Here the intertext seems

3. Nancy S. Hardin, "Drabble's *The Millstone*: A Fable for Our Time," *Critique: Studies in Modern Fiction* 15, 1 (1973): 293.

to do more than raise a character's consciousness; it creates expectations and channels the reader's response.

The concept of fate acquires prominent but precarious status in the opening paragraphs. Jane announces to her husband, Malcolm, that she would drown rather than resist fate by reaching out a hand to save herself.[4] Jane justifies her pathological passivity by a Calvinistic dichotomy between election and damnation: "Providence" will save her or not as it chooses. She has stilled herself into "some ice age of inactivity" (8), which she speculates may result from imagining herself a helpless victim.

Immediately we sense Jane's duplicity in her concept of fate. How would she know that "fate" wills her to drown and not to swim to shore? Her example betrays her passivity as a metaphysical rationalization of her will; she chooses self-destruction. She creates her life in the image of a story, an intertext of despair, that allows her immediately to identify with "the story of a pregnant woman, stranded by some unmemorable and unimaginable stroke of fate in a hut in the snowy wastes of Alaska" (9). The fate that stranded the woman in the story, Jane would like us to believe, also has stranded her alone, in a chilly London apartment with snow falling outside, about to give birth.

Our skepticism quickly finds corroborating evidence, for we learn that she has done quite a lot to alienate her husband and that she will leap at the chance to save herself when it suits her. Contradicting her initial proclamation, later she admits, "When offered a chance of salvation, I had taken it: I had not cared who should drown, so long as I should reach the land" (162). Her admission here falters, for instead of accepting full responsibility for her actions, she continues to blame fate for her nature and "what was to

4. Margaret Drabble, *The Waterfall* (London: Weidenfeld and Nicolson, 1969), p. 7. Hereinafter cited by abbreviation *W* and/or page number in the text.

be." "A fine evasion" she cynically, and platitudinously, adds, but this cynicism does not stop her from displacing responsibility onto an abstract concept of fate. Fate accommodates her evasive projection, for it can either mean what happens without our intervention or what happens because our interventions are predetermined.

Jane's fatalism invites the intertext of romance, in which love gains possession of the lovers not by their own design but by fate, by a force beyond human control. The lovers meet by fateful coincidence and feel helpless to resist their passion, even though it means the ruin of their lives. The intertext of romance cultivates a posture of self-fulfilling and self-justifying fatalism. Nothing convinces lovers of their inescapable plight more than stories about lovers in inescapable plights. Paola and Francesca, in Dante's *Inferno*, cannot resist bestowing fatal kisses on each other when they read that Lancelot and Guinevere did the same. Shakespeare's Juliet accuses Romeo of kissing by the book, but she loves him all the same. Frequently lovers within a romance realize the commonness of blaming fate for their love, yet they are not thereby dissuaded from doing so. Emma Bovary's recognition of the conventional phrases and of scenes of love only increases her determination to achieve the same, and she feels all the more justified in blaming fate when she is thwarted.

Drabble's Jane Gray often recognizes the conventionality of her story, yet she persists in believing in its uniqueness. She cites analogous love stories from literary history—Sue Bridehead, Maggie Tulliver, Jane Eyre—and then points out the difference in her situation. The narrative structure of *The Waterfall* embodies this denial of convention in its alternation between the supposedly "fictional" accounts in third person, which follow closely the tragic romance, and the supposedly "realistic" accounts in first person, which often attempt to undercut the exaggerations of the romance. Naturally, the denial of romance invokes the conventions of much realistic fiction, which defines itself through such an intertextual dialectic.

Drabble defends this alternation in point of view and between romance and realist intertexts by contrasting the narrowness of the experience of love with the analysis required to get at "the whole story" of that experience.[5] When Jane first breaks the third-person narrative illusion, she attacks it as prevarication:

> It won't, of course, do: as an account, I mean, of what took place. I tried, I tried for so long to reconcile, to find a style that would express it, to find a system that would excuse me, to construct a new meaning, having kicked the old one out, but I couldn't do it, so here I am, resorting to that old broken medium. (48)

Jane undercuts her initial style, implying that it was excessively conventional, not "new" enough. Even though she meant her love story to be entirely original, it has turned out that the "system" she created to excuse her adulterous passion was no more than the tragic romance, filled with commonplaces of literary precedent. She had previously invoked the myth of Cupid and Psyche to ennoble her vigil of love on the night James first shares her bed (37). One critic finds in this episode the intertext of Sleeping Beauty awakened by Prince Charming.[6] Jane's denial of convention cannot sustain itself against the tendency of romance to assimilate stories that emphasize its familiar form. Nothing assimilates stories more rapidly than romance.

Jane hoped her account, having "kicked out" the quotidian world of her self-doubts, would displace the need for realism. Now she admits her failure at rationalization through literary models and will resort to "that old broken

5. Peter Firchow, *The Writer's Place: Interviews on the Literary Situation in Contemporary Britain* (Minneapolis: University of Minnesota Press, 1974), p. 117; cf. Hardin, "Drabble's *Millstone*," p. 293.
6. Joanne V. Creighton, *Margaret Drabble* (New York: Methuen, 1985), p. 59.

medium," the language of the self she hoped love had displaced. The "old broken medium," we learn, also comprises multiple discourses: "the social view, the sexual view, the circumstantial view, the moral view" (49). Jane had wanted to escape the conflicting demands these discourses represent by suppressing all voices but the intertext of romance, but she could not maintain the suspension of disbelief. She now wants her rejection of the intertext to vindicate her choice of returning to realism.

Jane's denial of convention poses as a guarantee of truthfulness, disarming skepticism by acknowledging doubts and by confessing faults in anticipation. We find here the common convention of claiming realism by rejecting an intertext. Jane continues to follow this convention, posing rhetorical questions to the reader that seem to guarantee her reliability because they admit to the unreliability of her initial narrative: "it's obvious that I haven't told the truth, about myself and James. How could I? Why, more significantly, should I?" (49). We are intended to trust her because she must be honest to admit to being untrustworthy, and we have sympathy because fiction always falls short of the truth.

One particularly subtle pseudo-parody of romance conventions follows her claim that she had to suppress the truth, for "who could recount, without convicting herself of madness, the true degrees of love?" (49). This line parodies many poets, among them Shakespeare, who condemn lovers as madmen. But the parody is only apparent, for the line implicitly praises poets and lovers for being able to recount "the true degrees of love." So her parody, while it disarms criticism by acknowledging the madness of her discourse, reclaims the "higher truth" that only lovers and poets can know to be "realistic." Reading the following account of her mad tremblings and anxieties whenever James left her sight, we check our impulse to dismiss the report as exaggerated and Jane as a fool, for we have been warned that what was coming would sound strange but would be true wisdom. We recognize that this "higher realism" models itself on conventions of Elizabethan love poetry, which suggests the distinction in levels amounts to little more than different intertexts.

More generally, the narrative structure repeats this cycle of denying through parody in the first-person narrative the romance conventions exhibited in the third-person narrative, but then affirming that the romance conventions fulfill a higher code of realism than the conventions of the broken medium, realistic fiction. The first-person account finds many ways to disarm criticism of the romance version by speciously denying its methods. Jane maintains, it is "clear enough, in terms of narrative and consequence, that I would have loved James: what else could I have felt but love, for a man who showed love to me when I was so lost, so alone, in such abandon and distress? I loved him inevitably, of necessity" (52). Jane appears here to deny the romantic convention of lovers destined to meet and to fall in love by stating that the "narrative" was simply following psychological realism. She was in such great need, she would have loved anyone who came along; chance, not romantic fate, selected James. Jane then reverses herself and claims, "Of course it's not true, it could not have been anyone else. . . . it was a miracle, a stroke of amazing fate" (52). She now maintains that it would be a lie to deny the fundamental notion of the tragic romance, that the lovers were fated for each other, that they share a unique, miraculous destiny. What might have seemed outrageous if unprepared now seems plausible. Our skepticism of Jane's logic is disarmed by her apparent rationality. When she dispels that rationality and dismisses the conventions of realism with a claim of higher truth, we are that much more willing to believe her because we know she could be rational if she chose to be so.

The first-person narrator continues to earn our respect

for her rationality and realism. She reverses herself again, dismissing the terms and the conventions of romance: "Grace and miracles. I don't much care for my terminology" (52). Instead, she claims a concept of fate that recalls the Greek notion that "necessity" contravenes even the will of Zeus. But she congenially reverses herself again and robs fate of its austerity by saying first, it is "my God," and then, "Necessity lay with me when James did" (53). Her unvarnished truth here becomes entirely conflated with her romance. By equating Necessity with her lover, she implies that even though she has embraced the sternest possible religion of realism, she finds that fate, amazingly enough, really did bring her lover and "made him human, lovely, perishing."

Jane's first-person narration finds subtle ways of manipulating the romance formulas of the third-person account. She describes her parents' respectability, with their "faintly clerical background," and their disapproval of adultery. She smears them by comparing their social distinctions with those of Jane Austen (57, 61, 98) and claims much deeper feelings than they because she understands sexual drives and would choose Frank Churchill over Mr. Knightley (61). Her parents would be "finished" by "one straight look in [Jane's] face" (54). Having proved that she knows how "society" would "look" at her affair, Jane abruptly shifts tone to introduce one of the classical conventions of romance:

> When James looked at me, he saw myself. This is no fancy, no conceit. He redeemed me by knowing me, he corrupted me by sharing my knowledge. (54)

The sudden contrast in tone makes us credulous. Chilled by the icy tone of Jane's mocking description of her parents, we are all the more ready for the warmth of this first look, which, like the first look of lovers in romance stories, penetrates beneath the surface of their everyday personalities and reaches their inmost being. The contrast gives greater depth to Jane's description of James's look and vindicates her denial that it is a "fancy" or a "conceit" that the two lovers share a single transcendent knowledge of love. James both redeems and corrupts Jane: he redeems the buried love that society refuses to see, but he corrupts the repressive self that society does see. We want to be on the side that sees most, so we condone the corruption.

Jane knows that she cannot rely on such verbal maneuvering alone and that she must offer substantial reasons to prove the reality of her love for James. She tries to inject some "quotidian reality" into her narrative by discussing her infidelity to her husband (90). Not surprisingly, this part of her story ends up aping the logic of the romance intertext, subverting its claims of realism and objectivity.

"Love at first sight: I have heard of it: and like a doomed romantic I looked for it and found it, released into the air by the words of a long-dead poet" (92). Even Jane's account of meeting Malcolm reveals the inescapability of the formula. Jane is a "doomed romantic" because she has learned the intertext and follows its conventions when she thinks she finds them in reality. The cliché of love at first sight, "long rendered harmless to me by familiarity," thrills Jane anew when she hears Malcolm sing a song by Campion that "went straight to my heart" (92). Subsequent attempts to rationalize their love fail, and she admits their first look was the entire reason for her marriage. She indicts the poets, especially Shakespeare, whose Romeo and Juliet discover a fatal love in their first look (92). Her susceptibility to this intertext may indeed account for her romantic fatalism, but we expect a realistic first-person confession to find other sources of guilt.

The song by Campion that Malcolm sang combines the beauty of love with its outcome in a metaphoric murder:

> Then wilt thou speak of banqueting delights
> Of masks and revels which sweet youth did make,
> Of tourneys and great challenges of knights

And all these triumphs for thy beauty's sake:
When thou hast told these honours done to thee
Then tell, O tell how thou didst murder me. (93)

The Campion song "was prophetic," for its "lovely plan-gency" disarmed Jane, as it does the reader, and foretold the violence that doomed their marriage. Jane believed in the song, so she believed in Malcolm, not just superficially, as she would like to think, but in reality. She derides the song for trying to make murder lovely, but nevertheless she confesses that she prefers "to think of Malcom, innocent, passionate, singing of murder, than to think of him with his fingers and thumbs sunk into my shoulders, beating my head against the bedroom wall" (93). She denies the poets the right to beautify murder, but claims that right for herself. Her romance with James "murdered" Malcolm, but the romance justifies itself by the formulas of the tragic romance that exalt adultery. Jane recalls the now-familiar line from the song by Campion when describing how she drove Malcolm out of the house by physically and psychologically closing up against him (118). Did the song echo in her mind when she closed up? Did it excuse or rationalize her actions in her mind then, as it clearly does now, by an appeal to literary precedent? Or is the song, by coincidence having arisen and having prophesied the course of their love, merely the means she had of articulating the marriage's inevitable disaster?

The Campion song provides the paradox of beautiful cruelty that Jane and Malcolm's marriage enacts. Harsher versions of fate soon follow:

> In vain do I tell myself that there had been no hope, that he like me had been marked from birth for such a fate: the protagonists suffer and are guilty, though the drama is a drama of necessity. (94)

Fate again plays a double role here: first, it is denied as a delusive convention of romance, behind which Jane hides from responsibility; and second, it is reaffirmed, follow-ing the denial, as a drama of realistic necessity, against which the romance clashes. She admits that she and Mal-colm, like the protagonists in such a drama, are guilty, that the necessity does not negate their moral culpability. But finally her effort at self-condemnation proves vain and is once again swallowed up in the formulas of fate.

Later, when Malcolm threatens to return and to interrupt Jane's vacation with James, they rant at each other with lines that continue this drama of necessity: "I heard my own voice speaking as though I were another woman, a woman in a play, with lines that had to be spoken, in phrases that I had not known I knew" (186). Jane is not thinking of a spe-cific play but rather of conventions of drama inherited from general culture. Literature proves prophetic because it pro-vides preexisting vocabulary and structures for expressing emotions. Recognizing the intertext confirms her sense of fate, of living out a drama she has seen before and known for a long time was shaping her end.

As so many of Drabble's characters, Jane and Malcolm seek to escape their families in their marriage, but find to their chagrin that they both have inherited social ambition from parents. His parents' class was just slightly below her parents' class, which allowed for a fatal mix of social snob-bery and status-seeking. Jane realizes too late that her ro-mantic ideals have blinded her and that the drama of ne-cessity would be played out on its own terms, not hers. "Often, in jumping to avoid our fate, we meet it: as Seneca said. It gets us in the end" (103). Their belief in the escape of romance leads to fulfillment of the song's prophecy. The real imitates the literary, but not in the manner Jane and Malcolm first intended; fate confronts them with what had lain dormant all along.

Having failed by her discussion of her marriage to counter the tragic romance, Jane next decides no longer to resist, but rather to imitate freely the intertext of romance. Even in her first-person account, she says, her narrative will "re-constitute" her life, adding morality when it is missing, so she will have a "fictitious form" that will condone her actions (55). She admits that she risks "condemning all" (56) by falsifying part of her story, but she hopes that by admitting its falsity, we will see the integrity of her endeavor to tell the truth.

She tells the story of an "intimate question" James put to her one Christmas day many years ago, " 'What do you care for?,' " to which she replied, " 'Nothing much' " (70). She labels this "The narrative tale. The narrative explanation" and admits she left out parts so as to prove that James was fated to be her love, because he addressed to her "an intimate question on a beach on Christmas Day" (71). Their mystical intuition, contained in these rather banal questions and making their love unique, justifies her narrative manipulation. She claims that her love, not her conscious will, controls her narrative. This first-person account ends by describing how she drowns in the sea of her passion for him. "And so, if you would check, it ends in the same place" (71) as the opening third-person account (48), that is, no matter what she tries she ends with a dramatic image of her drowning in a sea of passion. Emily Dickinson, in the poem that Drabble uses as an epigraph to *The Waterfall*, links drowning with seeing the "Maker's cordial visage," which we shun "like an adversity." The image of drowning recurs often, and Jane recoils from it, finding the reality of its "death," like the reality of the sexual orgasm, appealing yet horrifying.

This also is the same point at which her following third-person account breaks off, leaving Jane and James happily to remember this moment of love as young adults, thinking of immersion into the sea as they descend below the Thames river into Blackwall Tunnel. The happiness evoked by this memory leads the first-person narrator to protest loudly, "Lies, lies, it's all lies" (89). Again we get breast-beating confessions and vows to tell the truth. And again Jane's method of truth-telling presumes upon its vows of honesty to justify its subsequent appeal to literary convention: "Reader, I loved him." The famous tag from Jane Eyre is perverted from "married" to "loved," updating the intertext and accentuating the adulterous, and therefore "tragic," nature of Jane's romance. Also, Charlotte Brontë used the tag to create a sense of closure at the end of her novel. Jane's narrative is far from over, indeed it never does achieve the closure "married" would indicate.

Jane puzzles over which man Brontë really loved, the man she could not have or the one she finally got. Jane tells us that the real man Brontë loved was the man of her imagination. It doesn't matter that Jane protests about James, "He was real, I swear it." Jane does not admit it, but we can see that she too has invented her lover; not the person but the story in which he finds a part. She has lived out the Brontë-like romance she so long envied by creating one for herself.

Jane accuses poets of lying about love, for presenting murder in terms of "lovely plangency" in order to disguise and to purify rejection, cruelty, and scorn. She cannot accept the lies of art, but she herself cannot cease to lie by seeking artistic purification and sublimation both in her narrative and in her life. Jane's own poetry at this time reflects the same dichotomy: beautifully shaped, with perfect meter and rhyme, but always about despair. Her art represses the deep unhappiness she feels by transmuting it to verse.

> The more unhappy I was the more I wrote: grief and words were to me inseparably connected, and I could see myself living out that maxim of literary criticism which claims that rhyme and metre are merely ways of regularising and making tolerable despair. (116)

Jane claims her poetry comes purely by "fate or chance" (116) against which passivity she struggles in her vain way to impose order by rhyme and meter. But this facade is transparent. The minute Jane's sex life improves, with James, she abandons poetry and picks up a "real" art, narrative romance. Although Jane wrote more poetry when she created distress and misery in her life, "grief and words were to me inseparably connected" (116–17), she also appears to be spurred on to write more narrative when elated by romance. In both instances, she creates the conditions for her art by imitating an intertext but then reverses herself and says the intertext distorts her life.

Jane's narrative, unlike her poetry, allows her to express her joy in finding a romantic passion. Perhaps for this reason her prose lacks the discipline and the control she claims her verse possesses (though we never see a sample). The form of her poetry becomes an intertext for her narrative, as it is held up as a contrast to her sprawling prose in the same way that her chaste and pleasant courtship with Malcolm is held up as a contrast to the sordid details of their marriage and her affair with James. The purity of delicately balanced phrases, like delicately balanced friendships—a "delicate ritual" she calls her relationship with James (143)— dialectically counterposes the continual obliteration of form created by her struggle to tell the truth. She would like to "write a poem as round and hard as a stone" (70) but always finds that words obtrude, reminding her of the painful need for human speech. Each time she says "I lied," we experience a messy disorder to her narrative, spreading itself out in ever more amorphous directions and forms to generate new oppositions between her art and life. These repeated admissions undermine all form by implying that any form distorts and may lie.

Jane asks, and we ask with her, what can be the relationship of the story she is writing to the story she lives. If she distorts and lies, does that distance the story from her real life? Or are her distortions necessary to approach the true form in her life? She constantly denies the reality of her story, but by telling us this she convinces us, presumably, to believe her story all the more. When she warns us that her account about Malcolm's desertion will be largely fabricated to protect herself but then goes on to blame herself, are we to trust the warning or her narrative?

Jane calls her third-person account "claustrophobic dialogue" and "schizoid third-person dialogue" (138). Literally, "dialogue" seems to refer to her conversations with James, but the nature of Jane's reference to "dialogue" makes it seem more an internal dialogue between contrasting sides of her psyche represented by the tragic romance and realistic, confessional narrative. The "dialogue" consists mainly of the first-person narrator loudly protesting the conventions of the third-person only to turn around and reinstate them. In the second first-person narrative (89–140), after accounting for her marriage and her relation to her cousin Lucy, Jane ends by saying, "One last concession I will make to facts before I return to them entirely" (140). In this strained, paradoxical sentence, the main clause implies the first-person narrator is our authority for facts, while the following subordinate clause implies that the upcoming third-person narration contains the facts, and nothing but facts.

Her "fact" turns out to be the recognition of a damning parallel between the love that she and James feel and that of another pair of romance lovers in Zola's *Therese Raquin*, a book James is coincidentally reading. That love was destroyed when the lovers killed the woman's husband, who ensured that their love would be adulterous and so conform to the tragic romance model. Like true lovers of romance, Jane and James read here, but fail to heed, a prophecy of their own future love, which depends on its adulterous nature to keep going. Which are the facts? The first-person literary allusion and recognition of the prophetic intertext? Or the third-person narration of love, carrying such intensity that we forget about this sign of their danger? Are facts to be measured by accuracy or persuasive power?

The third-person narration derives its power from the dream-world of romance, a world of "pure corrupted love" (138)—love outside of society's morality, but purely so and hence both moral and immoral. Jane's orgasm delivers her from the dry acerbity of her marriage, but her daily waiting upon James, the dark, menacing force that he is, floods her with desperate need. The description of Jane's orgasm bewilders the reader, intoxicating in its distilled physical ecstasy, yet awful in its violent passion (160–61). Joanne Creighton describes well the "narrative gamesmanship" that prevents us from settling on terms to describe their love.[7] Jane and James's game of bondage grows almost fetid in a grotto of love that could just as well come from *The Story of O* as from *Tristan*.

Freud keeps making an appearance to remind us of the neurotic patterns in Jane's guilty innocence, her confined freedom, her fixated progress. Freud explains that she wanted James because he belonged to her cousin, with whom she identified to the point of confusion (138). Freud explains Jane's unwillingness to put lids on jars, to interfere with organic decay, as justification for her utter passivity (154). Freud underlies her sexual salvation, which descends on her not like happiness but like some inevitable doom, expressing for Jane the savagery of human nature (161). Freud has taught us not to hope for release from our passions; like Maggie Tulliver in George Eliot's *The Mill on the Floss*, we are "abandoned forever to that relentless current" (*W* 163). (Drabble counters Freud by saying that the current leads us not just to "sticks, twigs, dry leaves, paper cartons, and cigarette ends" but also to "flower petals, silver fishes," implying that fantasy supersedes real-

7. Creighton, "Reading Margaret Drabble's *The Waterfall*," in *Critical Essays on Margaret Drabble*, edited by Ellen Cronan Rose (Boston: G. K. Hall, 1985), pp. 113–15.

ity [163–64].) Freud implicitly informs Jane's reference to Havelock Ellis's description of bondage in his "sexual text book" (163), which is a psychological equivalent for Isolde's love potion. (Again Drabble counters Freud by suggesting female perversions have not yet been treated as adequately by male psychologists as they have by novelists, citing Sue Bridehead in *Jude the Obscure*, Maggie Tulliver in *The Mill on the Floss,* and Jane's metaphoric drowning, [163–64].)

The lovers' exile from society, their "pure corrupted love," may entice us, seduce us as readers into suspending moral judgment. We may even allow that sexual catharsis warrants the price of psychological infantilism. But Drabble insists that the responsibility of a mother for her child will not accomodate itself to the tragic romance Jane uses to justify her neurotic withdrawal from parents, friends, work, avocation, and even excursions outdoors. More than once Jane worries about her effect on her children, and in these instances we do not find a witty intertextual play as we do in her self-lacerations about her husband and her cousin.

When Jane takes her children to the car racetrack to watch James speed recklessly and incompetently, setting himself in the posture of the hero of corrupt and dangerous love, she leaves him for a few moments and a remarkable change of perspective results (81–87). Her son Laurie finds some playmates, which relieves Jane because he will be away from her, and "she knew that because he was hers he was doomed" (83). She thinks of her nature as being handed down by necessity to him, that he is predestined to suffer a fate similar to hers (84). Similarly, when she thinks of sending him to a nursery group, she does so in what she fears will be a futile attempt "to break the fatal hereditary chain" (146). These thoughts lift us out of her claustrophobic desire for James and remind us that bondage has further consequences. Laurie naturally wants to break free from his role as Jane's "only contact with the outer world" (145). When she takes him to the playground or later to the nursery group, he responds quite nicely to the companionship of the other children, which creates a general brightening of mood.

Again, when James is absent in Italy and Jane wishes to create a diversion by taking the children to the zoo, she torments herself with accusation. Jane reminds us of her hereditary nature, saying that she is doomed to walk in a "fated pattern" in darkness (172). She hopes her love for James may have made her more willing to walk that fated path, less embittered, and so may have saved others from her worst nature, but she fears her terrible solitude, like "the dark contaminating stain," will kill and destroy her children (172). The zoo turns out to satisfy the children, though ironically the reward for her successful venture outside her claustrophobic world of desperate need is a postcard from James proposing a trip to Norway that awaits her at home.

The children stand outside the tragic romance, but Jane cannot concentrate on them, resisting the seductive pull of her passion. We naturally feel more empathy for the children as victims than we do for the outraged spouses, Malcolm and Lucy. Unlike Laurie and Bianca, Malcolm and Lucy seem partly to blame for what they get, for both have been unfaithful prior to Jane and James's affair. Nonetheless, the intertext demands moral confrontation between the lovers and those to whom they owe their loyalty, a confrontation that makes us waver between sympathy for the lovers and indignation at their immorality. Malcolm returns just before Jane and James leave for their trip to Norway to claim his rights as husband, but he ends up smashing the front window of her house, and Lucy calls Jane seeking companionship. Jane wonders "why fate had denied [her] the technical innocence of departing without a hearing of their rival claims" (192), but we know that fate to be the convention of the tragic romance. "Fate" denies her this innocence again when, after they have a horrendous car accident while driving to the Newcastle ferry, Lucy tells Jane she wishes she and James had both died (224).

The realistic narrative begins to merge with the romance intertext in Jane's confrontation with Lucy and Malcolm, as she no longer can distance herself with claims that her third-person romance contains nothing but lies. The car crash nearly brings the lovers to the fated end appointed by the intertext, a violent unity in death that follows as the natural consequence of their need to evade society's detection with stratagems that sooner or later are bound to fail. But they do not die, and Drabble emphasizes that the crash was not the consequence of their reckless passion, nor was it moral retribution. It was a freak combination of a loose brick, a blown tire, and a convergence of cars. The first-person narrator writes,

> . . . the accident, when reconstructed for me, was so horrific in its ghastly disproportion between cause and effect that it would have shattered any delicate faith: and yet how dreadfully it reinforced my views of providence, of divine providence, of the futility of human effort against the power that holds us. (197)

Fate, by judging the lovers and manifesting disapproval of their violations of social limits, comes near to convincing the first-person narrator of the validity of the tragic romance and the third-person narrator's fatalism. But despite its symbolic quality, the accident displays a "ghastly disproportion between cause and effect," manifesting fate's alternative aspect of formless and capricious chance.

Adding to the anticlimactic nature of the car crash, the absence of illumination at the moment when she thought she would die leaves Jane feeling cheated and betrayed (198). Jane expects wisdom will descend on her as do her poems, that is, without effort on her part. But she also fears this enlightenment, as does the drowning speaker in the epigraph poem by Emily Dickinson who rises three times before admitting the visage of her Maker. The car crash stops short of fulfilling the tragic romance partly because of Drabble's realistic displacement and her diminishment of the model, but also because Jane cannot yield finally and uncritically to the intertext that possesses her. Ironically, the crash will lead her to some enlightenment, though not as easily or as finally as she imagines.

Moreover, when she finds that James has not died from the crash, Jane thinks his death would have been much "simpler," "so natural a conclusion, so poetic in its justice" (201–202). Death would be poetic justice, for their love transgressed the legitimate possibilities of earthly happiness. According to the tragic romance, death transfigures and unites the lovers in a blissful state they could never achieve on earth. The intertext of romance would have her Tristan or her Romeo die in her arms, awaiting her in heaven as she desperately finds the means to kill herself. Instead, Jane compares the actual outcome to a contrasting intertext, one of meaningless suffering dragging on indefinitely, "like Gloucester, like Rochester" (202). She sees only the possibilities for unenlightened and unredeemed suffering, but her reference to these two characters ironically suggests her disillusionment may lead to enlightenment. Rochester, of course, reintroduces the tragic romance she will fulfill by attending James in his convalescence.

While these expectations of a climactic death show the first-person narrator to be an advocate of the tragic romance, her disillusionment makes her revert to mocking its conventions:

> The accident, it seemed, had given shape and form to my guilt: I could no longer evade it: I could no longer evade the dreadful assessments that crowded upon me, the comparisons, the judgements, the knowledge. Had he died, as all true fictional lovers die, had we both died, then these things would have been evaded forever. . . . (208–209)

Death would have been, at least in the fantasy of this first-person narrator, an escape from ordinary worries and jealousies through fictional transcendence. But James's survival vindicates the first-person narrator's rejection of the tragic romance conventions and occasions yet another claim of greater realism because she will tell the true story, including the assessments, comparisons, judgments, and knowledge. Once again a denial of conventions disarms our criticism and thus prepares us for a renewal of the lovers' dream.

The assessments, comparisons, judgments, and knowledge of guilt follow, but these are narrated in the third-person, not the first-person, which indicates a major shift in the relation of text to intertext.

> What on earth had they thought they were doing? It had been some ridiculous imitation of a fictitious passion, some shoddy childish mock-up of what for others might have been reality—but for what others? For no others, as non-existent an image they had pursued as God, as Santa Claus, as mermaids, as angels, as that non-existent image of eternity. A question of faith, it had been—but faith not justified by its object: love, human love. (215)

This mockery of the intertext of romance sounds like the first-person narrator. The voice that supposedly represents faith in eternal love here denies itself and becomes the self-critical voice of the guilt-ridden realist. Romantic love, the third-person narrator now claims, exists nowhere but in fiction, for unreal characters. They had indulged in a faith in this "fictitious passion," even risking the lives of her children, and now must face reality.

Jane continues for some time to berate James's as well as her own faith in romance: "Romantic love, that was what he had died for: how could he have allowed himself to be a martyr in so sick a cause, how could she have let herself accompany his suicidal fall?" (215). But he did not die, as she knows, and she must face worse doubts than simply the pointlessness of his martyrdom. She doubts the whole intertext of romantic love:

> How could she ever have trusted him and the lies they had told one another? How had they found so much to say about so great a delusion? The emperor's new clothes, discussed, endlessly, stitch by stitch: and suddenly one looks in the light of undeceived day, and the man is naked, like other men, and wanting like them nothing but what all men want. (215)

The tragic romance, which had previously made her trust James to rescue her, now gives way to the intertext of "the emperor's new clothes," a radical disillusionment.

Jane, in the third person, now admits that she and James were drawn together not out of a unique fate but out of "shallow stretches of ordinary weakness" and "past failures" (219). She sees the past "crumble to dust" (218) under the scrutiny of her new-found skepticism. She describes what they had truly shared as "an ordinary white rose, picked from a hedgeful of ordinary indistinguishable blooms" (219). She had learned the story of the white rose from watching television while waiting for James to recover. A princess wanted a blue rose, and many suitors tried to find one or to create one. But her true lover appears with a white rose, picked from an ordinary hedge, and tells her that it is blue. Like the princess, Jane wanted an ordinary romance that she could believe was transcendent.

Jane now has an intertext that, like the emperor's clothes intertext, displaces the tragic romance and acknowledges her new disillusionment but also indicates a willingness to find love despite this loss of illusions. The one remaining passage narrated in the third person (238–41) continues this attitude of reassessment and recuperation, treating briefly Jane's return to her house after James's recovery. She must clean up the mess awaiting there: physically in the form of broken glass and accumulated litter from the free-loaders who had camped there while she was away and emotionally in confronting Malcolm's petition for a divorce. She does clean up both messes and continues to love James, but under radically altered circumstances and expectations.

In the meantime, the first-person narrator returns and finds herself no longer at odds with her "schizoid double" third-person narrator anymore but rather with herself:

> I was hoping that in the end I would manage to find some kind of unity. I seem to be no nearer to it. But at the beginning I identified myself with distrust: and now I cannot articulate my suspicions, I have relegated them to that removed, third person. I identify myself with love, and I repudiate those nightmare doubts. (221)

The first-person narrator has ceded to the third-person narrator the role of doubting the tragic romance, which she now weakly embraces. She had hoped to find a dialectical synthesis, "some kind of unity," but found the "schizoid" third-person heroine as elusive and divided from her as ever. The third-person narration now represents the slow, patient hope for love to grow out of ordinary circumstances, while the first-person narration now represents desperate infatuation. The third-person heroine inevitably remains at a distance, being the fictional construct that, by way of a dialectically opposing intertext, gives form to contingency in the first-person narrator's life.

The first-person narrator feels this recrudescence of love for James, but with greater internal conflict than the third-person narrator evinces. Jane, as first-person narrator, sees "a vision of vast acres of growing things" when she notices some green streaks in the rushes making up her handbag (223). She hopes this is an omen that James is responding to her faith. But her cousin Lucy enters, sounding the note of "fate" and threatening to reestablish the claims of society on the lovers (224). Superstitiously, Jane thinks that when James recovers, he will return to her instead of Lucy if she just maintains greater faith. Jane invokes all "those tales of entranced lovers kept alive through the years by faith, those fables of sleepers and dreamers awoken finally by the intensity and endurance of desire" (230). She no longer parodies or mocks the conventions of romance, having too great a need for them to sustain her hope.

The first-person narrator cannot sustain the tragic romance, and the doubts she foisted onto her "schizoid double" reemerge. First of all, she mocks her fatalism, which had served so well as a cloak for her romantic fantasies (241). She mocks her pleas for clemency, for suspended judgment from her reader, and claims to accept guilt and responsibility for her adultery (241). From her present vantage point, her emphasis on romantic love was wrong; she should have been talking about guilt (242). She reminds us of her earlier belief in predetermination by repeating the aphorism: "In seeking to avoid my fate, like Oedipus, I had met it" (243, cf. 103). She now feels that to say things happen the way they do because of destiny evades the issue of moral responsibility; she admits to having contrived the circumstances that seemed to create an inevitable romance. She parodies the language of romance with her confession, "Those sick withdrawals had been nothing more than the sighs by which I summoned James to my side" (243). Her pose as "a woman on the verge of collapse, on the verge of schizophrenia or agoraphobia" was a lie (243).

But this denial of romantic fatalism only replays her earlier pseudo-parodies and her false denials of the intertext. She soon reverts to tragic romance, expecting her denial to have gained the reader's credulity. Once again she claims that James was "a miracle" that utterly transformed her life, thus extenuating her guilt in contriving her affair. She worships the gods of chance for having brought him to her, ignoring what she has just said about her own contrivance and manipulation (244). A compromise between these extremes, a synthesis of romantic fatalism and of realistic skepticism, continues to elude Jane, who seems capable only of oscillation.

Jane glorifies love through a comparison to a painting of a storm, which is owned, ironically, by Lucy's father. She believed love was like that storm, uprooting trees and gushing forth in "white torrential waters" (244). Her belief in love brought it about. "Had I not expected such events, they would not have occurred" (244). Her belief in love, in the intertext of romantic passions, constitutes her fate: "And so it is all fore-ordained, after all. I was merely a disaster area, a landscape given to such upheavals" (244). Jane's meeting with James, though outwardly coincidence, gained its power from her intertextual faith in romance: "what lovers have not believed that the whole of time has been watching over their convergence?" (244–45).

Jane does not seem here to have made much progress, first denying fate, then using that denial to contrive an affirmation of it. To achieve a true understanding of love, she will have to emerge from her cycle of accusing herself and then blaming fate. A glimmer of hope does shine from the renewal she feels in her life, which is symbolized by the green rushes in her handbag and the intertext of the white rose. She can find "no way to explain" this recrudescence of hope (245), which may indicate it avoids her preconceived notions of the tragic romance.

But the struggle continues because Jane's love still contravenes the marriage vows that society has ordained to channel passions. The tragic romance demands an irreconcilable conflict between passion and morality that can end only in tragedy. For Jane to renounce the tragedy and to construct an entirely different plot would be inconsistent with the dialectic of romance intertext and realistic denial that has guided her life and narrative thus far. She searches "for a conclusion, for an elegant vague figure that would wipe out all the conflict, all the bitterness, all the compromise that is yet to be endured" (245). Jane wants her narrative to make beauty out of pain as her poems do. But in this novel, the intertext of romance and the intertext of doubt reinforce each other. Jane searches for an image to express her assent to her fate, that is, loving James, but now foregoes all fleeting fancies of marrying him. Her passion exists largely because it violates social codes and, as with Zola's lovers, removing that violation would destroy the passion.

Jane considers revising her account, to make the accident conform more to the tragic romance:

> We should have died, I suppose, James and I. It isn't artistic to linger on like this. It isn't moral either. One can't have art without morality, anyway, as I've always maintained. It's odd that there should be no ending, when the whole affair otherwise was so heavily structured and orchestrated that I felt, at times, that I could see the machinery work, that I was simply living out some text book pattern of relationship. Perhaps the pattern is not completed: the machine, which throws up every month some new juxtaposition and some new reflection, is striving for an effect too huge to conceive, or for some finale too grand and too full of poetic justice to be approached without forty years of hard and intricate labour. (248)

This long and intricate passage summarizes key elements in the dialectic of text and intertext. The narrator cannot rewrite the story to have James die—a neat, "feminine" ending—because it would violate the pattern she has established of denying the romantic conventions. The pattern this time takes the form of saying, "But I hadn't the heart to do it, I loved him too much, and anyway it wouldn't have been the truth because the truth is that he recovered" (246). First she affirms the convention by saying she loved him too much; then she denies it by saying she is telling the truth, not a fictional story; and then she recants her realism, lamenting that it is not artistic, or even moral, to linger on. Though she doubts the intertext as a realist, she clearly yearns for its formulaic solutions as both artist and moralist. And as lover, according to this pattern, she must choose between an adulterous love and no love at all. Jane is doomed to live out the consequences of a passion that partakes of romantic desire, but a passion to which she cannot completely abandon herself.

Recognizing yet resisting the demands of tragic romance is a claim not just for realism but also for a higher kind of fatalism. She condescends to the "text book pattern of relationship she had been writing and living," mocking her own heavy-handed structuring and orchestrating, but she will not give up the idea of a machine generating her plot. Her recognition of the machinery at work prevents her from fulfilling the model; self-consciousness robs the passion of its unadulterated force. She needs to see her life patterned according to some intertextual design that will transcend her oscillations between the machine of romance and the stock denials of realism.

Here her limited vision of romantic fate verges on a grander, more inclusive Providential model. "Poetic justice" merges with biblical justice and the forty years of wandering and labor of the Jews. She pulls back immediately from such prophecy, for her irony cannot penetrate a model that in reality lies close to the problem she faces. She could only be reconciled with herself and could find a synthesis of her dialectically opposing voices if a final Judgment Day beyond her artistic control provided the image of conclusion she knows aesthetically her pattern demands.

Jane's inconclusive affair with James almost resolves "into comedy, not tragedy" (248). She decides to conclude with a description of a weekend visit she and James took to Goredale Scar, which she calls an "example of the sublime" (253). She describes this ending as "irrelevant" because the only "moral" it shows is that the romance intertext fails: you can have illicit passion and not pay the price; you can get away with anything (251). She has proclaimed that art must serve morality but clearly feels free to make an exception for the sake of realism if not passion.

Jane's denial of the conventional consequences of adultery is partly symbolically retracted, in their hotel room afterward, by an amusing drink of Scotch with talcum powder accidentally spilled in it. Their car accident could have ended in death with the odor of Scotch, the flask in the glove compartment having shattered and saturated the front seat with Scotch. The suggestion of love and death mixed in one drink comically parallels the love-death potion Tristan drinks with Isolde, which is usually described as magic powder dissolved in wine. Here we think we are getting a final synthesis, comic and harmless, of the tragic romance with realism: "A fitting conclusion to the sublimities of nature" (254).

But this novel violates intertextual expectations many times over, and we have not yet reached a conclusion. Jane's reminder at the end about the "price that modern woman must pay for love" (254–55), the side effects of birth-control pills, a thrombic clot, creates one final (this time it really is final) revolution of the wheel of passion and guilt. For one last time we are reminded of the intertext of romance, "In the past, in old novels, the price of love was death." This is not merely a comic parallel, however. Jane's adulterous, nonprocreative sex came close to killing her, and she still has not escaped all harm. She nods one more time to her philosophy of fatalism by saying her retribution is a good thing; she is guilty. But she then takes back her fatalism with a final, reluctant, impermanent, "I think."

Her final ambivalence typifies the problems that arise from her alternating attitude toward the tragic romance. On the one hand, she has embraced it, for it not only gave form to her passion but also actually seemed to create her passion at times. She loved by the "text book pattern." To follow this model passively, believing in fate, gives her a coherent sense of the world. But it also leads to real pain and suffering. Her acceptance of suffering as the inevitable, even the desirable, consequence of her romance would indicate a final concession to the power of fate and to a belief in moral retribution. Her hesitant "I think" suggests that such acceptance may contradict her emotions, which still demand the satisfactions of immoral love. She wishes to outgrow her fatalism but cannot.

Clearly Jane has achieved some progress, if only because the tone of the ending seems less neurotic, less schizoid than the earlier alternations between first- and third-person narrators made her appear. As Creighton has argued, Jane learns to live with paradoxes and disharmonies, not to seek wholeness.[8] Her recognition and incorporation of the intertext into her consciousness diminishes only the wildness of the oscillations, not their predictable recurrence. Jane remains conflicted between a fatalism her apprehension of the tragic romance instructed her to see and a rejection of the model her sense of realism demands. Her narrative is Drabble's boldest attempt at having a character struggle to gain explicit consciousness of the intertext governing her fate. But the passion Jane must experience overpowers her efforts at self-consciousness. Jane's narrative succeeds in diminishing the scale of this conflict but cannot hide its fatal permanence.

8. Ibid., p. 116.

III. The Return to Origin:
The Needle's Eye

T. S. Eliot, in *The Four Quartets*, tells us "the end of all our exploring/ Will be to arrive where we started/ And know the place for the first time." In our beginning is our end, and in our end is our beginning. The Roman personification of fate merged the goddesses of destiny with the goddesses of birth, implying that one's lot or portion in life is decreed at one's birth. Modern concepts of genetic determinism and psychological and social conditioning are not far from these ideas. Freud defined and formalized the universal impulse to revisit scenes of childhood, to establish a connection with one's origin, and to "read" the fate hidden there. The act of returning may be willed—one may choose to visit one's place of origin—but it may also be compelled—an unexpected confrontation with one's inheritance. In either case, and whatever the result, rediscovering one's origin will seem inevitable and will compel acceptance of the fateful influence one finds.

The return to origin operates more generally and indirectly in Drabble's *The Needle's Eye* than the tragic romance does in *The Waterfall* and will require a different conception of intertextuality. In *The Waterfall*, the tragic romance formed an obvious and explicit element of the narrative structure. Having a heroine write her own story and then comment on her writing naturally set up a dialectic between narrative models. In *The Needle's Eye*, we confront a situation of a character who lives out in realistic terms a more elemental plot paradigm, perceiving only some of its presence and rarely commenting on it. Furthermore, the return to origin has a wider, more diffuse literary tradition than the tragic romance. As a result, the parallels and the intertextual dialectic in this case will be somewhat less specific and much less explicit than in the first model we considered.

The Odyssey presents an ancient model of a homecoming, one illustrating the comic possibilities of renewal, although incorporating in dialectical opposition a tragic intertext. Throughout *The Odyssey*, Homer builds suspense by alluding to the homecoming of Agamemnon as a warning of what can happen to a warrior returning to a wife who has been beset by suitors. More generally, these allusions evoke the uncertainty of what one may find upon returning home, an uncertainty that will be dispelled by an act that seems only in retrospect to have been fated all along. In slaying the suitors, Odysseus arguably does not "know the place for the first time," that is, he expresses no new insight into himself as a result, but his victory centrally defines his character and serves as necessary prelude for reestablishing a connection to his birthplace and marriage bed. He must prove his identity to Penelope and to his father by telling stories and interpreting signs before his fate is complete.

Joyce constantly, but implicitly, invokes in *Ulysses* the Homeric version as intertext, using the correspondences to accentuate again the uncertainty of what awaits the hero upon his return home. Bloom "slays the suitors," after a fashion, by rationalizing to himself and telling his unfaithful wife stories of his adventures, calling to her mind memories of their earlier love. He also reestablishes his identity through recollections of his daughter and his dead father and son. The "realistic" conventions of Joyce's novel prevent Bloom from experiencing decisive victory or defeat; his fate is to live out a marriage that offers small rewards and much strain.

Marriage figures prominently in the return to origin, in direct antithesis to the adulterous love of the tragic romance. Marriage, though it may appear at first to be the means for escape from home, often constitutes the chief means for repeating and perpetuating the patterns of one's inheritance. In *Ulysses*, Leopold Bloom, musing on his courtship of Molly and her infidelity, thinks, "So it returns. Think you're escaping and run into yourself. Longest way round is the shortest way home." One's marriage repeats over and over again the logic of family history that led up to it. Thomas Hardy employs this model in many of his stories: Jude meets his fate at the end of *Jude the Obscure* by returning to his wife, Arabella, after recognizing that his attempts to escape his family's curse through his love for Sue Bridehead are doomed.

Often, too, a particular text will figure prominently in the return to origin, recalling the past either explicitly or by indirect association. Wordsworth's *Prelude* (Book 5) testifies to the permanent significance of a text known from childhood, its capacity for reawakening whole worlds of memories. Above all other texts, the Bible figures in the Western world as a link to childhood, home, and family. Texts or stories synecdochically convey not only particular associations but also general conventions about a return to one's origin. Bloom, unaware of the Homeric analogy he enacts, nonetheless thinks of fictional homecomings—notably the story of Rip Van Winkle—and makes up stories about himself as an eternal wanderer who, like a comet, returns after eons of peregrination.

Margaret Drabble uses variations on the return to origin in many of her novels. *A Summer Bird-Cage*, her first novel, opens with Sarah's experience of returning home after being in Paris. Clara, in *Jerusalem the Golden*, in a climactic homecoming, reads her mother's notebooks and discovers much about the origins of her family's conflict, but she fails to find a way to free herself from its influence or a way to redirect her feelings about her mother. Frances, in *The Realms of Gold*, reading the love letters of her dead great aunt, discovers a new connection to her ancestral home in the Midlands and rejects her previous fear of its depressing influence. She consecrates this connection by renovating her great aunt's cottage and living there with her new husband, Karel. Anthony, in *The Ice Age*, receives word of his climactic financial turnaround while he is at his parent's home musing in his father's parish, Crawford cathedral, about childhood rivalries with his brothers. Kate, in *The Middle Ground*, revisits her childhood home in Bromley and there meditates on the sewer smells she strongly associates with her father, who was a sanitation worker, and on the fairy tales with which she identified as a child in *Old Peter's Russian Fairy Tales*.

Except for *Jerusalem the Golden*, Drabble's early novels give sketchy pictures of the parents, family homes, and childhoods of the heroines. Intimations of their importance appear casually interspersed, for they have little impact on the plots. Rosamund, in *The Millstone*, and Jane, in *The Waterfall*, even joke about their parents' uninvolvement with their pregnancies and with other "family" matters. Correspondingly, in these early novels motherhood seems more a measure of the heroine's maturation than a theme of central importance for its own sake. *The Needle's Eye* introduces a much fuller treatment of both parents and children, connecting both in a climactic interweaving of plot in the scene in Branston Hall, the heroine's childhood home.

Thoughts of her home and visions from her childhood haunt Rose Vasiliou, reminding her constantly of her fateful pull back to her origins. When she finally does return to her family estate, her re-experience of some of her early conflicts and influences (especially by way of her memories of Bunyan's *Grace Abounding*) leads Rose to rethink her attitudes toward her ex-husband, Christopher. It seems at first a coincidence that her showdown with Christopher takes place on her family estate, but in retrospect we can see that this doubles the impact of her return to her origin, making it seem partly willed and partly an act of fate. Legal technicalities, newspaper stories, and complex logistics of phone calls and car rides all contribute an air of suspense with strong intertextual associations of melodramatic home-comings.

Freud looms large in Drabble's view of one's hereditary fate in her unraveling of this return to origin, just as he did in *The Waterfall*'s treatment of tragic romance. Drabble cites Freud often in interviews when speaking of fate and inherited feelings of guilt or depression.[1] In the beginning of *The Needle's Eye*, Rose and Simon meet at a dinner party and share their feelings of alienation from their homes, agreeing that it is sad but common to hate the place where one is born and not wish to return.[2] They also share a belief in hereditary woe, "that people endure not one lifetime but many, layers and layers of evolved suffering handed down" (23). As in *The Realms of Gold*, where Stephen Ollerenshaw's sense of Empedeclean depression surpasses Freud in lugubrious intractability, Simon, in *The Needle's Eye*, thinks of the 137th Psalm, about the sins of the fathers being visited on the children and being "worse than anything Freud had ever proposed in the way of predestination" (23). This general theme of inherited fate, transmitted through the family, takes more particular form in Freudian family conflicts: Frances's sexual rivalry with her mother; Simon's overly close, resentful attachment to his mother; and Rose's ambivalence toward her father. Simon thinks of Freud (along with Proust and Bergson) when he finds himself, like his friends who are in therapy, abusing his mother while musing about his wife.

Simon's reminiscences establish early in *The Needle's Eye* the importance of family and marriage in the fated return to origin and serve as background for Rose's later home-

1. Dee Preussner, "Talking with Margaret Drabble," *Modern Fiction Studies* 25, 4 (1979–1980): 567; Barbara Milton, "Margaret Drabble: The Art of Fiction LXX," *Paris Review* 20, 74 (1978): 62–65.

2. Margaret Drabble, *The Needle's Eye* (New York: Signet, 1969), p. 20. Hereinafter cited by page number in the text.

coming. In the very first scene of the novel, Simon, while buying a bottle of Vermouth, thinks about the woman in front of him in the liquor store and feels "violent waves of nostalgia possess him" (4), for she reminds him of his mother's impecunious, cramped life. The world she evokes lingers in his memory at the party, as he thinks of his host's similar social and geographical point of origin in the industrial Northeast. Nick has converted his lower-class background into a source of amusement for his rich friends, whereas Simon feels it is his "fate" constantly to suppress his resentment at the stigma of his origins, which increases his bitterness and melancholy (22). He instinctively thinks of his work, a defense that seems to him like a familiar journey, an attempt to create a new origin that conceals the old in a feeling of dull coldness (13).

These present thoughts engage the larger structure of return by establishing the principle that escape, through whatever defenses, inevitably fails, for one always meets a person or a situation that leads back to one's original fate. Simon thought during his courtship that he wanted to leave behind his mother's puritanical inhibitions by marrying a woman who represented to him "warmth, gaiety, vitality, family feeling, an easy affection, an easy enjoyment, all the things he had never hoped to have" (55). Given this background for Simon's marriage, the reader easily predicts Simon's subsequent disillusionment with his "escape." His wife, Julie Phillips, proves bigoted and cold, only superficially and defensively gregarious. Her own shaky social status (her father's mail-order business is slyly dishonest, though not actually illegal) has led to a "profound, irremediable crippling social ambition, founded on the insecurity of her own provincial background" (59), which exactly matches and exacerbates Simon's own ambition.

Simon recognized early on that their mutual attraction was an inevitable failure, two futile attempts to escape. But knowing the formula does nothing to stop its fulfillment.

He concludes that there must have been "in Julie a coarseness and a lack of discrimination that must have attracted him to her, as one is attracted, compelled, to approach one's own doom, to live out one's own hereditary destiny" (61). He recognizes that she will not be an escape for him, but he also senses that that is really her attraction for him, that he needed her coarseness to irritate the painful sensitivity he so unwillingly inherited from his mother:

> he had known, when, *at that point in time when*, he had offered to marry Julie, that he ought not to have done so, and that by doing so he was condemning himself and her to unhappiness. Why, then, had he done it? He had wondered even then, but there had seemed no possible choice. Inevitability had held him in its grip: psychological determinism had really got its claws into him. (63)

Fate here stands not for chance or for the whims of fortune but for the psychological determinism that, perversely it would seem, drives people knowingly to invite their own torment in their choice of marriage partner. In the metaphor of "claws" holding him we might interpret the intertextual image of the Erinyes, those classical furies that enforce a hereditary woe. Drabble implies that the "inevitability" gripping Simon could be interpreted as a Freudian conflict—marrying a mother-substitute while thinking he was escaping her—and also as a Marxist parable of class-consciousness—the conventional failure of bourgeois ambitions. He admits, somewhat later when thinking over the parallels between himself and Rose's social-climbing father, that he married Julie out of an endeavor to please his mother. She had "nourished dreams of escape" (118) first for herself and then, failing that, for her son, but he hated the sacrifices she made for his escape that ironically ensured his entrapment.

If knowing the paradigm did not prevent Simon from enacting it at the time, it does heighten his consciousness of his motivations for wanting to return to his home to make amends. Simon fantasizes such a successful return:

> There was nothing he wanted more, at times, than to drive down to [his mother] and to say, simply, I know now what you did, and I love you for it now, though I couldn't then: but it could not be said, it was too late, she would have to wait till her deathbed for such an acknowledgement. (119)

This deathbed acknowledgment is fantasy, but it is a structured and conventional fantasy common to the return to origin. Simon has a clear awareness of this clichéd formula, but his awareness only creates a self-conscious fear of uttering it. His failure to act out this role seals his fate as does Clara Maugham's failure, also as a result of inhibition at uttering clichéd words, to comfort her mother on her deathbed in *Jerusalem the Golden*. In trying to avoid one intertextual formula, both these characters fulfill the opposite formula of a tragically failed return to origin.

Mrs. Camish knows the return to origin as well as Simon, and to his great embarrassment she exploits it in simplistic, but commercially successful, stories. These stories, unashamedly nostalgic, evoke the hardship she had to endure while raising Simon as moralistic emblems of the virtues of fortitude. She even makes a quaint story out of her memory of her childhood outhouse (121). But while she will revisit her home in stories and clichés, she refuses to revisit it in fact.

Simon, willing to follow the intertext in this case, pursues his curiosity to see her childhood home in Violet Bank, which turns out to be a "grim and sunless," impoverished district (122). He finds renewal in his return to this origin, however. Drawn at first out of "fearful interest," fate, and "knowing himself compelled to knock at the door of the house in which his mother had been born," he meets an old lady there who tells him of the days when that area was covered with lovely flowers. He walks out into the street, relieved to escape this surrogate mother's chatter, but he is filled with

> a sudden apocalyptic vision, unsolicited, of the day when the world shall turn to grass once more, and the tender flowers will break and buckle the great paving stones. So recent they were, the days of green. Within living memory. And there would flow again the golden river, but there wouldn't be any people, waiting for the boatman. They would have gone, the people. Hell is full of people, but paradise is empty, unpolluted, crystalline, golden, clear. (123)

This "apocalyptic vision" of Edenic origins defines the intertext of the return to origin through biblical imagery and invokes the ultimate return at the end of time. As it was in the beginning, is now and ever shall be, world without end. Tender flowers will break up the paved confines and restrictions of civilization. The meek shall then inherit the earth. The Bible defines a grand intertext of homecoming that intrudes in the more local intertextual memories of phrases and images reminding Simon of childhood.

The future becomes the past and the present, as Simon goes on to think of the actual Violet Bank as having been "within living memory" an Arcadian setting. But he is upset by the notion that a restored Eden would have people in it. For Simon, Hell is other people, while paradise is empty, utterly beyond his experience.

Simon is caught in a puritanical trap, as Valerie Myer has pointed out.[3] He wants to disinherit himself from his guilt and anxiety, especially as they take the form of social ambition. Yet he reveals in his perpetual rancor "an eternal human pattern of corruption":

> This is it, he would think to himself, this is I, doing what all men do, I am enacting those old and pre-ordained movements of the spirit, those ancient patterns of decay, I, who had thought myself different. I, who had (surely) other

3. Valerie Grosvenor Myer, *Margaret Drabble: Puritanism and Permissiveness* (New York: Barnes and Noble, 1974), pp. 64–65.

intentions. Corrupt, humanly corrupt if not professionally so, and humanly embittered. And his spirit would struggle feebly within the net that held it, and he would imagine some pure evasion, some massive rent through which he could emerge. (126)

There is, it seems, no evasion for Simon, no renewal through a return to origin. For him the past remains a net, tenacious in its hold on him, limiting him to "pre-ordained movements of the spirit."

Rose has similarly strong associations to the past centered on biblical imagery, and she too will use these associations to heighten her consciousness of her fate. But for her the intertext does not inhibit action, despite her self-consciousness. As her name implies, she can experience to some degree a flowering, a rising, a transcendence of the present through a journey back to the past. Her middle name, Vertue, emphasized twice by characters remarking on its significance (46 and 74), also points to the Christian symbolism latent in "Rose." As a young girl she felt herself to be Jesus Christ reincarnated (74), and as a young woman she marries a man named Christopher, the "Christ-bearer." However, her religiosity as well as her marriage are mixed with inescapable conflicts, making her transcendence strongly qualified.

Rose has made for herself a fairly dramatic life, and her life with Christopher replays the extreme gestures and conflicts that led her to marry him. She frequently broods about the reasons for her marriage, wondering whether it was a foundation of truth and faith or a rubble burying her earlier, "priceless intuition" (76–77). She uncovers, during her ruminations, connections between the influence of her governess, Noreen, her marriage to Christopher, and her donation of a large portion of her inheritance. She tells Simon that Noreen trained her to fight against the materialism of her immensely wealthy family, to vow that she would not accumulate possessions which she would be afraid to lose (74–75). Her later attitude toward this vow is mixed. She enjoys the sense of moral purpose it gave her, but she also admits the folly to which it led. Her gesture toward disinheriting herself was a critical disruption for her marriage and reveals the depth of the conflict between her religious instincts and the influence of her origins.

Her marriage to Christopher offended all the instincts Noreen had so sternly cultivated:

> she had wanted him for so many reasons, all directly or perversely Noreen-inspired: because he was sexy and undeniable, and crude about it, and anybody less crude she would have been obliged to deny—but with Christopher one abandoned judgement, one fell, hopelessly enchanted, into whatever mud or gutter or dark corner or creaking second-hand bed that one could find—that was a perverse reason, a reason that rejected Noreen (as she would have had to be rejected, because she herself, Rose Vertue, could never have made much of a virtue of chastity, as Noreen did, she was not made of the right kind of flesh or spirit) but there were other reasons more directly descended, though Noreen would not have liked to acknowledge them as her offspring. (79)

Rose perversely rebelled against the rule of chastity by finding such a crudely sexual man. Her puritanical guilt would not let her accept easily the attractions of sex, so she validated her guilt by marrying someone who violated her limits of decency.

Rose casuistically manipulates Noreen-inspired teachings of the puritan doctrine of meekness and sympathy for the dispossessed to justify her rebellion—was not Christopher one of the dispossessed? Rose inverts this puritanism again when she shouts Noreen's doctrines to Christopher during arguments mired in blood, violence, and social snobbery. Like Simon, who deceived himself in thinking that consciousness of his motives would safeguard against falling into a foreseen trap, Rose's understanding helps little in averting the effects of puritanical repression.

Rose had wanted her marriage to Christopher to free herself entirely from the conflict between the influence of Noreen's religiosity and her parents' materialism, but she finds, as did Simon, that her choice of marriage partner confirms, through guilt, rather than denies her bonds to her past. When her parents separate Rose from Christopher, she thinks her worst fate would be to be alone (109), but she later thinks, "Fate had not separated them, they had swum the Hellespont" (111). This intertext of romantic love ending in tragedy counterpoints the attenuation of Rose and Christopher's love. "The spirit bloweth whither it listeth," one of the many biblical tags that pack Rose's mind, intrudes several times in reference to the dying of love in her marriage.

But if their love cools and fades away, their intense battle with each other only increases; "it was a fight in which there was no winning" (182), no matter who won in court. Rose thinks later, "What freakish providence had given her Christopher, so obsessed by the thought of possession that he refused to let her reject him" (333). His is the will to possess, hers to renounce. She had wanted her marriage to free her from her father's materialism. But in an ironic twist of fate, Christopher turns out to embrace Mr. Bryanston's doctrine and even to become a close friend. Rose saw only the outward rebellion, without realizing that Christopher, in rising from rags to riches with somewhat shady business practices, was of the same kind as her father, whose manufacturing business skirts the edge of the law. Thus when Rose shouts at Christopher Noreen's anti-materialistic doctrines, especially the biblical parable of the rich man entering heaven being like the camel passing through the eye of the needle, she uses the very words of rebellion that once had led her to marry him.

To escape this fatal repetition of her family's conflicts, Rose seeks to dissociate herself entirely from the Bryanston estate in Norfolk, which she tells Simon she hates even if she likes it too (20). Her new dwelling on Middle Road—an obscure, run-down, middle to lower-middle class section of London—promises a new origin, one based on her religious values of simplicity, of being in the "middle." Like Simon's vision of Violet Bank, Rose's house provides a vision of renewal,

> a hope for the future: she shivered, she trembled, she flinched, but she persevered, she had faith, she built up brick by brick the holy city of her childhood, the holy city in the shape of that patched subsiding house. (53)

This "holy city," strongly reminiscent of the the imagery in *Jerusalem the Golden*, represents paradoxically both the long journey she has made since leaving her parents' house and a renewal of the happiness she found in isolated moments there. The reality of the present slowly, through careful work and great patience, merges with the ideal of a timeless restoration of childhood fantasies of escape from her parents' materialism. Unlike Simon, Rose finds in the past hope for the future.

Rose builds this "holy city of her childhood" brick by brick, out of ragged, frayed, dilapidated furnishings. At times irritated and at times attaining a "visionary peace," Rose forms an alliance with the objects around her that "irradiated her, transformed her" (54). "Hardly a gleam" of her vision reaches others, making us at first doubt her achievements.

But Rose proves herself to Simon and, through him, to the reader. Simon visits Rose at her home one afternoon and sees her with her friend Emily, who shares with Rose a scrappy, weathered look that nonetheless reveals a "blossoming" of good will (213). Simon admires their completeness. The women of his experience mostly conform to stereotypes, to two-dimensional images, whereas Rose and Emily are people with a history, having made themselves through much deliberate effort.

Simon discovers in them a vision of possibilities, confirmed when they visit a bombed-out, nearby lot that is inhabited by chickens and a decaying armchair claimed by a "feathery dusty old hen" (216). At first Simon resists this vision of objects restored to beauty by Rose's willed poverty; he sees instead the meanness of mass-produced and cheaply built houses and furniture. But with the sun shining after a rainstorm and with Rose's influence, he sees some charm despite the tawdriness.

> So great and innocent a peace possessed him that it seemed like a new contract, like the rainbow after the flood. He could feel it, on his bare hands and face. It lay upon him. It was like happiness. (216)

Unlike Simon's earlier vision following his visit to his mother's home, this apocalyptic vision does not end by rejecting the intertext of biblical renewal. The future promises to restore some original purity, the inadequacies transformed by a "covenant" to a pledge of redemption. For about the only time in his life, Simon manages to let this peace possess him without self-conscious, cynical undercutting.

The outing stirs memories for Rose of her girlhood friendship with Emily, the person most capable of appreciating her attraction to simple, natural objects. Rose had started a collection of pressed flowers to stave off boredom, but no one else besides Emily seemed interested. From this flower book sprang a conversation about how boring life was, and from that conversation sprang a feeling of happiness and joy, the memory of which continues to give pleasure many years later. Rose has since shared her book with her son, Konstantin, who finds it equally enchanting and who generally shares Rose's fascination with flowers and with abandoned objects (219). Through a "text" of pressed flowers, Rose shares her deepest feelings about her childhood with her son, transmitting a hopeful fate to counter her guilt. In *The Waterfall*, Jane shared some similar moments with her children, but she could not build on them by connecting her present self and her children with her childhood and by forming a family commitment deeper than her rebellious passion.

These objects and the memories they evoke for Rose capture the essence of the desire for simplicity that has been a constant in her life, counteracting her parents' luxury. When Rose was four, Noreen had introduced her to the village school, which she liked far more than her later private tuition (106). One of her teachers, Miss Acomb, had a box of pictures from around the world that charmed the youngsters because of their "primal simplicity" (108). Rose's memory of this school, and the books and buildings, forms the basis of her attempt to re-create the "holy city of her childhood" in their present home:

> it was a world that she had hoped her own children would find, here, in this brick desert, in this dense and monstrous urban wilderness. It had been a foolish hope, a ridiculous expectation, but it had been justified. They had found it, it was there. (108)

Rose, in her isolated world of urban poverty, has transmitted to her children a sense of the radiance of common objects and of life that she rescued from her own childhood and re-created for them. No doubt much of Drabble's description of this simple world comes from her own childhood experience at a Quaker school,[4] reflecting the Friends' emphasis on simplicity and the presence of God in each person, however humble.

Christopher calls and disrupts the mood of peace Rose has found in these memories. His call seems to Rose a reminder of her fate: "like a punishment for having thought that she could be happy. As now indeed she no longer was" (223). She thinks often of Christopher's continuing hold on

4. Joanne V. Creighton, *Margaret Drabble* (New York: Methuen, 1985), p. 19.

her and on the children as "a penalty" and "a judgement" (179). Noreen disturbed her peace as a girl, as Christopher does her peace as a woman and a mother. Rose allows these two individuals to draw her into acrimonious battle because she feels so guilty and undeserving that her happiness and peace seem a crime. She knows there can be no release from this fate through divorce or through other legal separations: "There was no solution, through violence or law" (181).

Fate, in the form of psychological determinism, binds Christopher to Rose and destroys the possibility of her continuing in the peaceful world she has managed to create for herself.

> That dim surging and conflict within her when she thought of him and what they had been through together could not be parcelled out or judged or ended by any means but its own. In its own place it must be decided. (181)

Rose must accept that "in the human spirit there was depth, there was power, there was a force that would not, could not accept any indulgence or any letting off. Struggle on it would, because it could not rest, it could not say, forgive me, I have had enough." The narrator hyperbolizes, but the personification of this force allows us to imagine why rationality fails to prevail. Of all Rose's friends, Simon comes closest to persuading her that she has a moral and legal right to her peace. He sees in her the grace he lacks of looking to the past for renewal, so he finds it doubly painful to see that her past has another story to tell, one even more insistent than his own. The hostilities buried in Rose's rejection of her parents erupt in her conflicts with Noreen and Christopher, leaving her simplicity and peace permanently disfigured.

At first, we see Christopher entirely through Rose's eyes as a social-climbing wife-beater. We cannot believe he married Rose for any other reason than her money, and we cannot see why she married him, except from sheer desperation. We hear about him only from Rose, and, like Simon, we naturally take her side. But about halfway through the book, Christopher's fatal stature grows through a series of elaborate parallels and coincidences. When Simon and his family spend a holiday at Cornwall, he imagines that he sees Christopher with the three Vassiliou children (189–91). It wasn't them, but the vision of him with the children stirs Simon's mind. Perhaps he unconsciously recalls on this Easter weekend, as Drabble surely intends the reader to do here, the story of St. Christopher, who carried the Christ-child on his shoulders. When Simon returns from Cornwall, coincidentally the first person he sees is Christopher with the three children, who are delighted by Christopher's new Jaguar. "He had known that it was coming: the false shadow in Cornwall had been a portent. It would have to be dealt with, this new dimension, and there would be worse to come" (205).

Worse does come. The plot becomes more dramatic, as Simon and Christopher begin to square off for a battle that keeps being deferred. Though his ogre-image begins to erode, this Christopher is still no saint. When they meet at a party shortly after Easter weekend, Simon is not surprised, for "he had known it was coming" (224). He begins to see the bond that ties Christopher to Rose, and to himself, as a force not to be resisted, as fate, when he sees that Christopher in fact is Rose's spiritual counterpart, sharing her irrationality far more than Simon ever could:

> He had known it for certain, when he had seen the false Christopher with the child on his shoulders, in Cornwall. How could he have supposed such an image to represent Christopher, if he had not been afraid of the very truth? And later, on his return, seeing the real Christopher with the children in his car, he had known it all, in his heart. (232)

Simon fears this truth, which he has suspected all along,

because to admit Christopher's sincerity, to believe that he did not merely marry for money, would be to admit that Rose belongs with him. She does belong with him, an idea that increasingly dominates Simon's thinking and thwarts the romance conventions that have created expectations of love fulfilled between Simon and Rose.

Suspense builds and can only be released through a confrontation between Rose and Christopher, but the confrontation must also be between Rose and her family, against whom she rebelled in marrying him. Christopher accomplishes this confrontation in one of Drabble's most carefully plotted sequences. He realizes his plan to win the children back through a legal suit will never work, so he attempts a melodramatic maneuver to shock Rose into seeing things more his way. Drabble adds to the suspense with several intertextual analogies, most significant of which is the news story about an Italian father who, on losing custody of his child in England's Court of Appeal, abducted the child to Italy (267). Christopher plays up this intertext by sending Rose a telegram stating that he is leaving England with the three children, whom he has in his possession for the purpose of taking them to the Bryanston estate in Norfolk.

In a surprise move that can be explained only through the return to origin, Christopher takes the children to Norfolk anyway and makes no attempt to abduct them. Following much legal wrangling, Simon and Rose chase after him, and they seem at that moment on the verge of a breakthrough in their relationship. Simon, legal guide and reassuring male, rescues Rose, desperate mother and susceptible companion, promising to restore her not only to her children but also to her sense of trust. Christopher has set a trap, perhaps knowingly, by having the rescue scene take place at Rose's home. She expects to disengage herself from him finally and irrevocably there, but the past interferes.

On the way to Norfolk, Simon asks Rose, "'When did you last see your father?'" (288), and "they both laughed at the classic question." The question is classic in several ways. It is the title of a painting by William Frederick Yeames, painted in 1878 and reproduced very widely in English history books as a moral emblem.[5] It depicts an upright, aristocratic lad facing a slouching, motley group of rebel inquisitors during the English Civil War. The question implies that the boy will never see his royalist father again, but despite their intimidation, the boy remains steadfast, unlike his weeping mother and sister behind him. The allusion humorously, if incongruously, emphasizes that Simon and Rose face a tense situation.

The question is also classic in the clichéd sense of a psychoanalyst probing a patient's feelings about her father. Simon, the knight in shining armor, now becomes a threat to Rose's complacency, inadvertently raising troubling issues. The cliché surfaces because in fact the situation strongly resonates with overtones of adultery. For Rose and Simon to be taking a long drive together (leaving Simon's wife, Julie, in the lurch for a party they had planned to attend and outwardly defying Christopher) implies a new level of connection. Furthermore, for Rose to be taking Simon to her father's home suggests the paradigm of courtship. Simon senses this new dimension and follows up his first classic question by inviting Rose to meet his mother.

A more somber note is struck when they stop to look at Rose's personal forest, an Eden of which she has been unable to dispossess herself, and they walk into a dangling, dead stoat, "mummified, dried out by exposure, archaic, pagan" (295). The stoat frightens and appalls them, but it also allows Simon, through a surprising Freudian association, to voice a sentiment he has been harboring for some

5. John Sunderland, *Painting in Britain: 1525 to 1975* (Oxford: Phaidon, 1976), pp. 249–50.

time, "'If I had been free, I would have asked you to marry me.'" At this "classic" line, they both stare at the corpse and lament the past. The symbolism almost verges on self-parody, but the intent is serious. The reader now recognizes a change in the plot; we will not see Simon and Rose form a new, living thing during this homecoming, but we will see their romance wither—not disappear, but mummify. The car trip in *The Waterfall* accentuates the romance intertext, but this car trip emphasizes the displacement of that model by the return to origin.

When they arrive at Branston Hall, Simon and Rose find a need to defend themselves against the powerful emotions aroused by her homecoming. They pose as picturesque tourists visiting a "National Garden," which is coincidentally open for its annual afternoon showing on that particular day. Rose even says, "Perhaps I could disguise myself. I don't know why, I always knew I'd come back one day in disguise" (296). She "disguises" herself by putting on Julie's sunglasses and headsquare, adding further innuendos of their intimacy by taking the place of Simon's wife. Rose continues the intertextual play by saying, "'We could have a recognition scene, later, in the drawing-room or the library or the rose garden.'" The recognition scene she has in mind refers to conventional scenes of romance and comic theatre when true identities are finally revealed, errant lovers restored to families, and marriages culminate all in happiness ever after. Unwittingly, she prophesies the submerged intertext of recognizing her own identity as a result of her return to her origin.

Rose's identity begins to emerge for Simon from the incongruity of her "modest features and her unassuming spirit" with the flashy headsquare and grand estate. Simon thinks,

> nature had made her unremarkable, an ordinary person: fate
> had capriciously elected her to notoriety: and she had made

the painful journey back to nature by herself, alone, guided by nothing but her own knowledge, against the current. (299)

"Fate" plays a double role here. Insofar as it stands for social conditioning and family wealth, Rose's return to her origin pits her true identity against her fate. She finds her way "back" to her true nature by building a substitute home in her shabby London dwelling. But this estimate is Simon's, who idealizes Rose and consistently sees only this side of her character, considering it her pure self unfortunately contaminated by others' influence. He fails to acknowledge that fate also elected her to notoriety, that part of her self is capable of splashy gestures of rebellion.

Christopher sees and brings out in Rose the side Simon represses. When the showdown occurs and the three encounter each other, the melodrama reaches grandiose dimensions, suiting the aristocratic setting. For Simon, it is "too much, too much intended" (300), as he experiences the meeting in slow motion ("as though time had broadened endlessly to describe it"). The intersections of the garden seem to him like "intolerable pretensions of those who think themselves free to operate," like the "landscapes of the idle soul." For Simon, the garden resembles an operatic or theatrical "set" "built, designed centuries ago, for confrontation." He sees himself enacting the melodramatic role he had hoped to avoid and wants to deny in Rose. Christopher, however, stands back smoothly, composedly, and takes her in with aplomb.

Rose bends quickly under Christopher's influence:

> really, she thought, in the end, one had just got to take him, and that's that. Her spirit, for the first time in years, moved to acceptance: she felt it embark for that final flight, she imagined it might one day rise and reach and settle in the clearer air. (304)

She senses that she would achieve her true transcendence, her flight, only through accepting Christopher, who seems so full of life next to the embittered Simon. She thinks later:

> Ah, Christopher. One could think what one might think about Christopher, but at the very least he had filled in the time. He knew how to stave off boredom, did Christopher, he knew how to keep things on the go. (332)

But before Rose can accept Christopher, she must reenact those scenes of the past in which she rebelled against her parents and Noreen, for they were the origin of her need for him.

Rose first relives her feelings toward her parents during dinner. Simon sees the overbearing crassness of her father and the morbid querulousness of her mother, and he naturally wonders,

> Where had [Rose] come from, how had it happened? People do not grow out of nothing, they do not spring from the earth. Somewhere in this house, in these two disagreeable ageing people, in this dingy dining-room, lay the grounds for her fantastic notions. He felt almost as though there must be some spirit, some clue, hovering in the air around them. Perhaps it was the spirit of desolation that hovered with dark wings and a vacant spiritual gaze over the polished wooden dining-table. It had brooded over her, as a small child, it had blessed her and inspired her. (311–12)

Simon describes Rose's return to her origin here as a rediscovery of a "spirit of desolation" that had inspired fantastic notions of virtue. He understands well how strong this spirit can be and has learned to appreciate her virtue, which is why Rose derives such satisfaction from his modest desire for her.

Rose confirms Simon's impressions, finding dinner with her parents "dreary, oppressive, painful beyond belief. Hearing her father talk business was like some old record replayed" (315). She knows the intertext of the return to origin, the formula of reenacting the past to achieve renewal, but she finds her encounter with her parents mere repetition. She recognizes in them aspects of herself, like her mother's hypochondria and her father's inhumanity, yet she also feels again her cold need to reject these aspects. She does not feel worthy of transcendence, yet that was her fate.

Christopher rises in her mind as a possible source of "grace," for he has managed to encounter her parents and has actually "given to her father's image a pale gleam of hope" (315). Yet she now recognizes from her experience in coming home that this hope was illusory, that there can be no mitigation of her cold hostility toward her parents through Christopher, despite his close relationship to his father. Realizing this, she feels compelled to travel further back in time, to reexperience the influence of her earliest rebellion.

"There was always Noreen to be remembered" (316). Rose "had a sense of some appointment more significant than confession, which awaited her upstairs" (323). She feels now, and has felt throughout the book, her fate drawing her toward this encounter with the past, inescapably forcing her to return to the scene of her greatest fears. Outside the door of Noreen's former bedroom, Rose "felt that a step more would take her across the threshold of time itself, into the dreadful past" (324). Here, more than at any other time, Rose appears conscious of the intertextual role she plays in revisiting scenes from her childhood.

Rose does enter Noreen's room, and she composes the scene as if deliberately maintaining an aesthetic awareness of conventions; by recognizing her feelings as formulaic, she discovers her fate. As in many Victorian novels, the governess holds the long suppressed clue to her identity. She calls forth Noreen's "ghost" and feels as if she is transported back in time, with the present "dissolving" from around her, and as if she is entering down the long "corridor of memory." She recalls a scene from when she was six in which she tested one of Noreen's pronouncements, that razors "would cut you as soon as look at you" (327). The razor blade had cut her, and so Rose became convinced that Noreen was right about everything she said. Rose experiences again her desperation in face of Noreen's threats and asks the words she had been trained to ask, "What can I do to be saved?"

At this, the climax of her return to origin, Rose sees the text from which her question came and is drawn into the final stage of the intertextual model. Bunyan's *Pilgrim's Progress* had, when she was a girl, given her comfort by acknowledging the seriousness of the need to be saved. Rose finds next to the book Bunyan's autobiography, *Grace Abounding to the Chief of Sinners*. She had learned these works by heart, so glancing at only a few fragments calls forth the whole. They stand synecdochically for years when Rose, caught between miserable parents and an equally oppressive salvation, would pray to die. She finds in this book a birthday card she had planned to send herself on her fifteenth birthday, reminding her of how lonely and abandoned she had felt. But the card also reminds her that she had recovered; like Bunyan, she had endured the Slough of Despond and found her way to the "state of grace" she has enjoyed ever since she met Christopher (332).

Rose has found in her return to her origin the connection she had suppressed between her recovery from despair and her attachment to Christopher. She remembers a significant moment with him, on the last night she had slept in her parents' house, when among the flowers in the garden she had felt transfixed by "a silence, a stopping of the blood in the middle of the evening" (332–33). Her discovery of sexuality with Christopher forged a bond to him that countered Noreen's harsh religion, and it provided an alternative form of rebellion against her parents.

By rediscovering this story of her past, Rose frees her feelings to turn more toward Christopher and her children.

Before she returned to Branston Hall, she had bought her serenity at the price of repressing the violent connection she had forged with her husband, a connection that in more ways than just the biological one had made the children possible. She had come close to acknowledging this bond before, when suddenly she was overwhelmed by a desire to return the children to Christopher and by a vision of Noreen beckoning her to go to Africa. At that time she could mock, through an allusion to a painting of the day of judgment, the histrionic quality Noreen inspired in her (265). But then she still maintained the illusion that she could win her battles by withdrawing from the field of conflict, thinking that was how she had won battles as a child. She was wrong in this, which helps explain why she could not rest with her legal victory over him. Nor could she have simply given the children to him, for he would ruin the purity of her self-sacrifice.

At Branston Hall, chance and deterministic fate converge during a farcical ménage à trois in the corridor. Caught off guard, Rose returns to the embattled role she has played so often with Christopher. Instead of saying she was checking on the children, she says she was avoiding him (337). This, she thinks, is "a fatal admission—fatal to admit that she was aware that he might have been looking for her, fatal to admit that even so dim a connexion might still exist." Fate has found her out by chance, by necessity, and forced her to recognize that her spirit still pushes her toward the somewhat degrading marital battles she had so often tried to escape.

Christopher had helped her to escape her home, but when love faded, her battles with him had returned to the hostilities of her past. She now is forced to realize, as a result of her experience in returning to her origin, that her battles with him were inescapable parts of her humanity, her scruffy, scrappy humanity. Her ideal of pure self-sacrifice and plain living is part of her life; with Emily and Simon she proved it so. But with Christopher her histrionic, embattled nature comes out. Once admitting this aspect, she inevitably feels less secure in her rejection of him; it is a fatal admission.

The connection grows the next day, as Christopher intends. He virtually arranged the melodramatic sequence at her parents' home, evidently trusting to luck, knowing that he could strengthen his hold on her in that context by reliving the past battles he had won. At one point during their outing to the beach, the oldest child, Konstantin, eagerly hopes his Dad will buy a yacht. Rose becomes furious at Christopher's use of material ploys to win back the children's affection and implicitly to repudiate Rose's legal victory in gaining custody.

> There it was, in a nutshell, their domestic life. Rose, distorted by rage from all her virtues: Christopher, idly provocative. Simon felt a chill in his bones: he shivered. (346)

This tableaux summarizes the fatal change that takes place at Branston. Rose's virtues make her rage all the more fiercely at Christopher's complacent yet stubborn indifference to her morality. He forces her back into a position of Noreen-like rebellion and denial of life. Yet she must, from her nature, choose this battle rather than Simon's detachment. Perhaps if she and Simon had formed a bond when she had first needed to break out of her isolation, both of them would now share the strength of emotion she shares with Christopher. But as it is, Simon has subsided permanently into frigidity, and she must replay endlessly the disillusioning failure of her "escape."

Several years later, Rose wrestles with her ambivalence about her decision to remarry Christopher (364–65). She regrets the loss of the solitary, but calm, spiritual purity she had when living alone with her children. True, elements of her experiment in simplicity remain and bear fruit. "Fate" intervenes on Rose's behalf and makes her neighborhood rise in status, thus ensuring her continuity there and vindicating her faith (357). She has a job with the British Council working for the development of Ujuhudiana, fulfilling, albeit more conservatively than in her first attempt, her mission to the people of that country. But overall, she feels her life with Christopher, even though it has been on her terms and in her house, has ruined her nature, made her constantly ill-tempered and peevish. She wishes she could say that she enjoyed the strife and the nasty arguments, but she cannot deny her feeling of relief whenever he is away.

Rose concludes that she accepted Christopher back out of religious duty, for the children. But the children are, while important, not her main motivation, for she cannot persuade herself that they really are better off with Christopher and her yelling at each other and at them all the time. She imagines her soul tormented by Christopher and longs for transcendence in the "warm daylight of love" (366). This transcendence can come only from silencing "the harsh clanging of her own voice, the sounding of righteous brass and the clanging of the symbols of her upright faith-demented ideologies."

She learned from her trip to Branston Hall a lesson she partly represses because it is so painful, the lesson that she will never silence these voices of religious battle. She does have the charity Paul wrote of in I Corinthians, but only in part. The sounding brass and tinkling cymbals (symbols) were her family conflicts as a child, and she discovered on her return home that they necessarily remain with her in her marriage to Christopher. She had thought she would escape them with him, and when that failed she tried to re-create "the holy city of her childhood" in Middle Road, free from her inner torments. The very real transcendence she

74

achieves in this endeavor, through moments of relief that she can find in simple things and with her friends Simon and Emily, grows in value even though those moments are subsumed within her larger, conflicted fate.

This ideal self, so attractive in its virtue, is not Rose's true self, as some feminist critics think. Ellen Cronan Rose sees Rose's remarriage to Christopher as a "regressive" capitulation to the "patriarchal institution" of marriage, a female denial of self in response to his male power. Marion Vlastos Libby concludes, "A female trapped once again with a hostile man, Rose is inevitably at odds with her true, her human self."[6] Such an embattled posture disowns Rose's aggressive behavior and, like Simon's belief that her true self is all simplicity and grace, denies the inner conflicts that lead her to fight her father and her husband with self-lacerating gestures. On the other hand, it would be just as wrong to sentimentalize Rose's return to Christopher as reestablishing the family as a "haven" of "warmth and safety" opposed to the "harsh real world" around them.[7] Rose no sooner accepts Christopher than she fights him, both when they first marry and even more so when they remarry. Rose's fate is to reenact this cycle perpetually, gaining all the while an almost heroic identity from her acknowledgment of its inevitability.

Drabble has given critics grounds for questioning this inevitability, suggesting that Rose might have been mistaken in taking Christopher back[8] and that they probably "would part again after another five years because she

6. Ellen Cronan Rose, *The Novels of Margaret Drabble: Equivocal Figures* (Totowa, N.J.: Barnes and Noble, 1980), p. 87; Marion Vlastos Libby, "Fate and Feminism in the Novels of Margaret Drabble," *Contemporary Literature* 16, 2 (1976): 191.

7. Mary Hurley Moran, *Margaret Drabble: Existing Within Structures*, Crosscurrents Series (Carbondale: Southern Illinois University Press, 1983), pp. 75–76.

8. Drabble, "The Author Comments," *Dutch Quarterly Review of Anglo-American Letters*, 5 (1975): 37.

couldn't take it."[9] But Drabble also asserts that the novel creates a logic demanding that Rose remarry Christopher.[10] This ambivalence reflects the harshness of the intertext of the return to origin, which seems in this case to eliminate Rose's choice to build on the moments of grace that have ennobled her struggle and have seemed to legitimize her freedom. Drabble plays with this intertext, making Rose largely unconscious of its implications. Yet she does fulfill its terms and so embodies the cultural norms she has tried to fight.

The final scene at the Palace dog show contains multitudes of possibilities: transcendence—temporary, of course, but radiant in dust and in tattered fur—as well as decay, disfigurement, and vulgarity. What gives the scene, like the mass-produced concrete lions, identity is not an essential nature, but accident and erosion. Certainly Rose could have chosen differently and might thus have retained a certain wholeness. But the choice she did make becomes her fate and creates what Nabokov would call a harmony with chance. Her acceptance of this fate—she does not attempt to create a false clarity and sense of freedom—widens her personality and increases her stature even though it does not attain a final transcendence.

9. Nancy S. Hardin, "Drabble's *The Millstone*: A Fable for Our Time," *Critique: Studies in Modern Fiction* 15, 1 (1973): 285.
10. Drabble, "The Author Comments," pp. 37–38.

IV. THE PROVIDENTIAL MODEL: THE ICE AGE

The Providential model embodies a religious sense that God has ordered the world according to a plan that will someday be revealed. Usually beginning with a state of crisis or despair linking the guilt of a hero with the ills of society, stories following this model progress through seemingly chance events to an end that reveals an aesthetic and moral design that expiates the initial state of woe and proves it a just penance or a trial of faith. Providential design may remain a mystery, though at some point the story expresses a faith in its ultimate manifestation: things may not make sense at the time, but they will someday.

Fate plays an ambiguous role in the Providential model, referring alternately to chance and to design. What at first appears to be chance, often to the character's horror, turns out to fulfill a foreordained design. In a religious sense, this design ultimately coincides with God's Providence, though the word *fate* may at times resist this interpretation. Boethius, in *The Consolation of Philosophy*, distinguishes between fate and Providence by saying that both denote the manifold rules by which all things are governed, but while Providence pertains to these rules in relation to divine reason itself, fate pertains to them only in relation to mutable things.[1] Providence is the unfolding of temporal events as viewed by the divine mind; fate is the resolution of these same events as viewed from the human perspective of time. Fate often appears as chance in the mundane world while nonetheless serving the purpose of an unchanging divine will.

---

1. Boethius, *The Consolation of Philosophy*, translated by Richard Green (New York: Bobbs-Merrill, 1962), p. 91.

The narrative equivalent of the religious sense of fate draws upon the Latin word *fatus*, meaning that which has been spoken or decreed. Being foreordained need not contradict chance or free will, though this is the familiar paradox of predestination. What appears mutable when enacted may well seem immutable and predestined in retrospect. The Providential model assumes such a double vision and generates a plot that employs much chance and coincidence yet results in a simple design overall. Although any plot creates a tension between initial ambiguities and their unfolding significance, the Providential model explicitly reveals this tension to be universal.

The Providential model is a general intertext, in some ways subsuming all other intertexts of fate. It asserts that the shape we find in life is borrowed from previous stories and fits somehow into a universal story. In one sense, fate may simply be one's lot, neither moral nor purposeful, as inexplicable as the roll of dice. But even calling one's lot "fate" defends against incomprehensibility by giving the illusion of naming a pattern. Such an epithet claims a coherence: "fate" implies shape to life, often despite obvious contradictions. By labeling a sequence of events "fate," we impose a beginning and an end onto diffuse and contingent circumstances.

In pre-Christian times, a sense of Providence usually was associated with moral retribution for past crimes or for fatal flaws. Oedipus is spurred on to discover his crimes by the divinely ordained plague that creates great suffering in his land. What at first seems strange and bewildering becomes clear once the link between his guilt and the plague is discovered. The discovery (in Sophocles's version) results from a coincidence, the simultaneous arrival of the shepherd who abandoned Oedipus as a baby and the messenger who found him. Chance here achieves a fateful design, just as it did earlier when Oedipus, despite his determined effort, encounters his parents. Finally, the plague relents once Oedipus has accepted responsibility and paid for his crime.

In Christian times, and especially from the seventeenth century onward, Providence is less often seen as punishing crimes than as testing a character's faith and rewarding constancy. Dickens begins *A Tale of Two Cities* with a story about the Woodman "Fate" making a guillotine, setting the stage for the inevitable and prophesied revolution. Immediately following this parable, Dickens shifts to a story about a mysterious messenger intercepting the Dover mail coach. At first, one can see no connection between this messenger and the French Revolution, but later a link is revealed and the promise of the Providential model is borne out as *A Tale of Two Cities* unfolds the complicity of chance with fate: the right characters turn up to save the faithful hero in the nick of time. The ending transforms "the best of times, the worst of times" into a promise of redemption by a savior. Also, imprisonment, a key motif in the Providential model, figures prominently in Dickens's novel. The righteous are in prison at the beginning, enduring a test of their characters if not their faith, and the guilty aristocracy are imprisoned at the end (along with some other righteous ones, of course).

Margaret Drabble's novels usually present suffering as a test of character, vindicated by reference to family relations. The character who most clearly fails this test, Jane, in *The Waterfall*, operates within the contrasting romance model, in which to succeed in passion is precisely to fail in terms of commitment to family. Among the other early novels, characters succeed more or less (Rose and Rosamund more, Sarah, Emma, and Clara less) in making of their suffering a test of their devotion to children or family. Only in Drabble's later novels, beginning with *The Needle's Eye*, does family commitment become explicitly generalized as a metaphor for the state of society at large. In *The Realms of Gold*, Frances establishes her family's strain of depression as a symbol of a social malaise partly inherited and partly influenced by the flat, midland landscape. Fate and chance conspire to transform this depression into renewal, though some characters succumb to their imprisoning attitudes and never escape.

The Ice Age invokes the Providential model by opening with a sense of doom—a financial depression hanging over England combined with revolutionary terror that seems comparable to the opening of Dickens's *A Tale of Two Cities*. Kitty Friedmann, having lost a leg as well as a husband from an IRA bomb, begins her letter to Anthony Keating, "These are terrible times we live in." The epigraphs to the book oracularly guide us in identifying these signs as conforming to the Providential model: Drabble quotes Milton in *Areopagitica*, describing England as an eagle rising up from sleep, and Wordsworth, pleading for Milton's prophetic vision to inspire the present dire times with hope. Drabble is too much a realist to expand this theme with a Dickensian allegory, but she comes close in her opening paragraph.

A pheasant dies of a heart attack and falls into Anthony Keating's pond, recalling his own nearly fatal heart attack and seeming like an omen of divine displeasure. The narrator defends the plausibility of a pheasant's dying of a heart attack ("as birds sometimes do"), but this defense merely calls attention to its improbability and allegorical import. The dying bird gives Anthony "cause for some dark reflections." He was saved from death by the caprice of fate: even though it would be more common for a human to die of a heart attack than a bird, he was spared and the bird was struck down.

The book ends with Anthony, in prison, naturally, gazing at another bird, a small tree creeper that "rarely visits below the snow line, rarely visits the haunts of men, a secret beauty."[2] The two birds stand to each other as type and antitype, confirming the Providential model; the end is contained in the beginning, and the apocalyptic overtones of the opening presage the melody of renewal at the end. Anthony calls the tree creeper "a messenger from God," a promise, an angel. In place of a dying bird, we get a soaring, singing one, a portent of hope, joy, and life, fulfilling the design prophesied by Milton's eagle.

All England does not rise up in *The Ice Age*, and Anthony's experience of renewal takes place tantalizingly removed from our vision, but the model does define the overall structure. *The Ice Age* allows design slowly to emerge from contingency. Part one sets forth the depression troubling England in general and Anthony and his friends in particular. Part two defines a slow, halting improvement in Anthony's physical and financial health and a corresponding deepening of his sympathy for others. Part three presents Anthony as having found a faith in God through suffering imprisonment and through rediscovering the significance of art (playing guitar) and nature (bird-watching). But to sketch this overall design in the plot makes the intertext seem one-dimensional, whereas Drabble's text manipulates it in sophisticated ways. Anthony's recovery comes in two not wholly compatible stages (parts two and three) and often seems unrelated to the general state of England.

Right from the start, we are led to doubt the link between Anthony's situation and some universal necessity or design. Anthony broods over a series of misfortunes and concludes, "There was no one common cause for all these terrible things. Or if there was, [he] had not yet grasped it" (7). This invokes the intertext of the Providential model but questions it in the name of realism, creating a suspense about the possibilities of a final revelation that will iden-

2. Margaret Drabble, *The Ice Age* (New York: Knopf, 1977), p. 295. Hereinafter cited by page number in the text.

tify "one common cause." Anthony may never grasp the cause, yet we expect the narrator will give the reader the satisfaction of seeing the pattern emerge. At the very least, we expect to see some of the reason why Anthony cannot grasp the interconnectedness of the seemingly random accidents.

Similarly, when the narrator, referring to the terrorist's bomb that killed Max Friedmann and maimed Kitty Friedmann, asks, "Why Kitty, why Max, why Anthony Keating? and why had the punishments been so unrelated to the offenses?" (6), we expect an answer to emerge. Is Kitty's lameness retribution, a test, or merely chance? If it is a test, Anthony thinks, "there was no possibility of her failing the test, God had wasted his time, maiming Kitty" (7). We find out later that Kitty was not so infallible; she escaped despair and loss of faith simply by avoiding conflict, somewhat as Anthony has done by retiring to seclusion in his new and inappropriate country manor. She also connects ironically to Anthony's father's ministry, for her generous innocence "little resembled the Christian patterns of virtue [Anthony] had been reared to admire" (7). However, these connections never develop, nor is Kitty's husband's death ever linked to Anthony.

Drabble plays off the intertext when she calls Anthony's problems a "neat" case of "poetic justice" (9): he had been caught in a trap of his own making, overreaching himself physically and financially, thinking he could outsmart the market. The whole point of the Providential model, as the narrator assumes we know, is to hold in suspense any explanations until the crisis unfolds. Calling Anthony's collapse "poetic justice" at the very beginning of the story short-circuits our expectations of puzzlement. We know it cannot be that simple.

The narrator restores the anticipation generic to the Providential model by mocking the "poetic justice" she so abruptly reveals. Anthony wishes to "survey the disaster from a more detached position," from which the "poetic justice" would be aesthetically pleasing, "but it is hard to be detached about one's own debts" (9). The narrator here undercuts the "poetic justice" she has created by calling it too "literary," the form being too neat and the distance of a narrator from her story being too secure to serve as a model for Anthony's life. We expect an explanation that, while borrowing its form from literature, will not be merely a literary narrative formula. Providence must be revealed more "realistically" and must make Anthony's suffering part of the general crisis afflicting England.

Parenthetically, the narrator adds, "poetic justice" cannot explain Max Friedmann's death, for he had been exceptionally prudent, unlike Anthony, in his investments. This further mocking of poetic justice implies that this story is realistic because it presents cases that do not follow the conventions of poetic justice. But on a more general level, this question raises doubts: why should one individual receive poetic justice and not another? These questions assure us that Drabble's narrative structures itself on, even while it resists, the Providential model.

This parenthesis also suggests that the interconnectedness of all these disasters is subjective, governed more by Anthony's present state of mind than by an objective pattern. Earlier, in commenting on Anthony's response to the dead pheasant, the narrator suggested something similar: "It gave rise to some solemn reflections, as most objects, with less cause, seemed to do, these solitary and inactive days" (3). Does this subjectivity create an irony about his "solemn reflections"? Perhaps there is no general crisis, only individual ones that conform to no universal pattern.

The narrator continues building on the ambiguities of the crisis: "even the heart attack had not been the final blow aimed by fate at Anthony Keating" (11). Is the narrator mocking Anthony here? Or parodying her own rhetoric? Are we to take the phrase less seriously, as simply a colloquial way of referring to bad times? The "final blow," we are told here although there are many more blows to come, is the arrest of Alison Murray's eldest daughter, which will turn out to have much greater significance than first appears. The arrest forestalls Anthony's marriage to Alison and ominously suggests that their marriage may never take place. Furthermore, the arrest will provide one tangible link between Anthony and the state of England as his attempt to rescue Jane becomes embroiled in political conflict. The Foreign Service calls on him to attend Jane's unexpected release from prison and to deliver some secret papers. "And that was how Anthony Keating became a British spy" (257), in the narrator's hyperbolic phrase, and perhaps in his own.

Drabble's narrator maintains this self-mocking tone throughout *The Ice Age*, alternately distancing her "realistic" story from the paradigm of Providence and implying their coincidence. The word *fate* usually appears in clichéd, pretentious phrases that nonetheless turn out to signal crucial developments of plot or of character. Anthony's financial crisis is compared light-heartedly to that of his friend, Linton Hancox, who teaches Classics at Oxford: "the fate of classical studies might, like the fate of the property market, indicate something of a watershed in British history" (72–73). This reference to a "watershed" introduces a serious parallel, despite the playful tone. The comparison of Anthony's fate to Linton's, as well as to England's, echoes in Anthony's later musings about the "three fates" that lay hard hands on Antigone. Anthony has just read Linton's introduction to his translation of *Antigone*, which compares her plight to the irrational and violent present, while he is embroiled in a turmoil of partisan battle at the Wallacian airport (283–84; cf. 223). The "watershed" begins to take on more tangible form.

Similarly, when Anthony escapes serious consequences for his financial speculation, the narrator comments, "By any law of justice, he, like Len Wincobank, should have ended up in prison, or like Max Friedmann, dead. But fate had given him a second chance. Yet again, he was going to have to decide what to do with his life" (225). This playful reference to laws of justice and to prison acknowledges the whimsical quality of fate in a light-hearted tone and then insinuates the serious test of Anthony's character. We are as baffled as Anthony at his good fortune, and though the comparison to the plight of his companions yields little sense of universal justice, we can tell that Anthony's case by itself will conform to the Providential model.

Other references place more emphasis on the fickleness of fate, highlighting that aspect of the plot in contrast to Providence. Alison explains Anthony's drinking bout following his financial rescue by thinking that "Anthony was an emotional man, a man of spirit, who would not sit quietly beneath the blows or benefactions of fate" (233), which implies a moral relativity governing Anthony's fortunes. As Jane escapes from Wallacia but Anthony, for no obvious reason, does not, the narrator describes Jane's plane as rising, "leaving Anthony to his fate" (279). Anthony summarizes this capricious aspect of fate by contrasting it with a Miltonic or Boethius-like divine plan in making him endure such a trial of faith (again referring to *Antigone*): "he cannot bring himself to believe in the random malice of the fates, those three gray sisters. He is determined, alone, to justify the ways of God to man" (294).

Fate plays a double role, at times suggesting a universal design—suffering as just punishment or a trial of faith—and at times suggesting morally indifferent whims and caprices of chance. Drabble extends and amplifies this doubleness in small, off-hand references to fate. When Maureen Kirby returns from a visit to her former lover Len Wincobank, who is now in prison, "by some unpleasant trick of fate" the car radio plays the song about the prisoner returning home who wonders if he will see the yellow ribbons signifying his lover's fidelity (128). This coincidence is both a "trick of fate" and a symbol of Maureen's inner struggle against the temptation to be unfaithful to Len. Len, for his part, worries about the chance of his trees being struck by lightning and calls this possibility fate, which is in part a symbol of his anxiety about Maureen's fidelity (163).

Len's worry about the fate of his trees is more than matched by Tom Callandar, a fellow inmate and former financial wizard, who believes that something has gone wrong with the laws of chance. His view might be intended to parody the Providential model, for he believes in a conspiracy threatening him and his friends that would account for everything from lightning strokes and airplane crashes to inflation, IRA bombs, and, naturally, the imprisonment of his friends. Len thinks Callandar is mad to connect so many different things together, yet in adding up the misfortunes having befallen himself and his friends, he has to admit that he is puzzled (167). Callandar's view of a conspiracy is parodied for its extremism and its obvious self-justifying motivation. But Len and the reader have sympathy for Callandar's mad search for an underlying order despite the infuriating reminder of how close to madness lie his universal explanations and connections.

Directly contrasting Callandar's externalization of blame is Alison Murray's internalization. For the most part, Alison believes "there is no such thing as an accident. We are all marked down. We choose what our own ill thoughts chose for us" (155). She uses this notion of self-victimization to explain various tragedies in her life, primarily her sister's breast cancer, her daughter Molly's cerebral palsy, and her older daughter Jane's bicycle accident. Her theory holds some merit in the case of Jane, who suffered the accident immediately after Molly stole Alison's attention from Jane. But she realizes, as does the reader, that exaggerating her guilt can be her form of evading the harshness of

86

fate. Alison thinks, "No, one must continue to behave as though one believed in the accidental. That shows our greatest faith. Molly's fate is an accident, not a retribution" (155). Her efforts to objectify guilt meet with very limited success, and she continues to blame herself neurotically. Though she does becomes severely depressed, she does not go insane, and we feel, even more strongly than we do for Callandar, a mixture of sympathy and unease at her notions.

Alison further reflects the Providential model when she sees time not as "consequential" but as occurring "simultaneously," a loose collection of experiences from which we select our own patterns among spots of sorrow and joy (247). A series of tragedies is the fault of bad selection, not the general situation of society. Alison cannot believe her own theory, for she has suffered too many "blows of circumstance" to believe one can find comfort if one wills it. Her choices hardly seem enviable: obsessive guilt for every misfortune or self-pity for being a victim of fate. Still, both choices have the advantage of a neurosis, of controlling and ordering experience, thus assuring a predictable structure to her life.

The Providential model forces us to question along with these characters, pondering what, if any, connections exist between various instances of suffering and whether there might be a single cause for the clusterings. The book's structure embodies these possibilities by setting forth a large number of simultaneous events and by calling attention to the lack of an obvious causal relationship. Part one develops the situation of a dozen or so characters on a given Wednesday in the second half of November. In a characteristic parody of her methods, the narrator admits that her selection of characters and situations has created an exaggerated pattern of depression, but she maintains that, nonetheless, it really was almost that bad (59). Part two begins by informing us of what these characters were doing on the following day, Thursday, the nineteenth of November. Another sequence of segments (161–68) defines these characters' situations during a severe thunderstorm a few weeks later, and yet another sequence of segments (183–92) describes their activities on Christmas of that year.

Sometimes these groups of segments are internally linked by one character thinking about what is happening at that time to another, as when Len thinks of Maureen, who is thinking of Len while she is dining with Derek. Sometimes thematic parallels are made between situations, such as Anthony's weakness in returning to drink and Maureen's weakness in starting an affair with her employer once again. Sometimes the simultaneity seems utterly gratuitous, as when we are treated to a list of minor characters and told how they spent Christmas or to some characters we never meet (187).

The effect is dizzying at times, as we spin around trying vainly to see all of what is happening at a given moment in England. In part one, after describing the general depression of so many characters, the narrator declares, "This is the state of the nation" (63), clearly parodying her own pomposity and indicating the futility of such generalizations, though by her mockery anticipating criticism and thus retaining some substance to the claim. The narrator makes a similar pseudo-parody of her own method when describing Maureen Kirby as "by much the nicest of this perhaps unrepresentative group of British citizens" (189). Such comments seem attacks on the novel form and make us wonder how closely the story will follow the Providential model in finding by the end a single shape for the disparate lives of its characters.

The significance of this method of simultaneity, and a more satisfactory view of Providence than Tom Callandar and Alison Murray offer, begins as Anthony responds to the comedy routine of his old college friend, Mike Morgan. Following Mike's challenging question, "So what next. What do you prophesy, Giles?," and the ensuing silence, Anthony muses, "To what an end we have come" (221). *End* here clearly means both termination and goal and reminds us that the method of simultaneity resists any notion of ending. Nonetheless, there can be moments when the whole seems comprehensible, when the larger picture emerges unexpectedly. Anthony experiences such a moment:

> it seemed to Anthony, as he sat there listening to the silence in the room, and the creaking sounds of London, that there would be an answer, for the nation if not for himself, and he saw, as he sat there, some apparition: of this great and puissant nation, a country lying there surrounded by the gray seas, the land green and gray, well worn, long inhabited, not in chains, not in thrall, but a land passing through some strange metamorphosis, through the intense creative lethargy of profound self-contemplation, not idle, not defeated, but waiting still, assembling defenses against the noxious oily tides of fatigue and contempt that washed insistently against her shores. An aerial view, a helicopter view of this precious isle came into his head, and he saw the seas washing forever, or more or less forever, around the white and yellow and pink and gray sands and pebbles of the beaches, this semiprecious stone set in a leaden sea, our heritage, the miles of coast, as yet unenclosed, not yet roped and staked and parceled. What next? The roping, the selling, the plundering? The view shimmered, fragmented, dissolved like a cloud. The silence lasted. (221)

The allusions in this passage (to Milton's vision of England as an eagle in *Areopagitica* again and to Gaunt's description of "this scept'red isle," "This precious stone set in the silver sea," "This blessed plot, this earth, this realm, this England" in Shakespeare's Richard II [II.i.40–60]) remind us that literary models help us make the panorama of history conform to a single vision, the "aerial view."

Rather than trace single lines of cause and effect, the text endeavors to encompass the whole country, envisioning patterns of Providential design that transcend the view of the individual. Needless to say, this intertext of a panoramic view is also a prop for self-parody. Like Milton and Shakespeare, Drabble articulates this view of England's potential as a critique of the present, playing off their images with ironic phrases: "oily tides," "helicopter view," "semiprecious stone," and "more or less forever." Also, the silence of the view is shattered by a gunshot right outside the window in the street below: "Because it was London and not New York or Detroit, they assumed it was the backfiring of a car rather than a gunshot, and did not much react" (221). The irony mocks Anthony's vision of the whole, for he fails to grasp what lies right in front of him, much less the future of all England. Still, the irony is not total, for Anthony's effort here reflects the book's method of simultaneity and the pattern of "metamorphosis" it attempts to depict in his career.

Anthony's vision partly reflects his faith in himself; he is undergoing his own metamorphosis "through the intense creative lethargy of profound self-contemplation." By the end of the novel, he does attain a vision transcending his earlier, morbid introspection. By suffering, he reaches self-understanding and vindicates Providence's challenge to his faith. How much his resurrection has to do with England's remains a critical problem with the book, which indicates a dialectical opposition, in the name of realism, to the Providential model. But insofar as the paradigm does apply to Anthony, the misfortunes and the setbacks he endures are typical of his generation and are justified in the end by his faith.

The dominant image for these misfortunes is imprisonment, both for Anthony and for many of his friends. Len Wincobank, the businessman who so impressed Anthony that he left his liberal views and secure position with the BBC to speculate in land and property development, shocked Anthony by being put in prison for fraud. Anthony meditates on Len's example, as well as on Jane Murray's plight in jail in Wallacia for her car accident, finding in their punishments a sobering analogy to his own situation. Len and Jane learn a little from their imprisonment; Len vows not to make any more mistakes, though we may infer he will continue his corrupt business practices, and Jane seems somewhat chastened and even grateful to Anthony for coming to get her. Humphrey Clegg, the minister from the Foreign and Commonwealth Office, acquired a transvestite obsession from a maid who dressed him up as a girl when he was little, and now he is "imprisoned by this misfortune in a jail from which there would be no release" (258). While the degree of guilt and rehabilitation varies for each, these prisoners form a background for Anthony's imprisonment.

Though mainly the result of chance, Anthony's final imprisonment seems predestined in light of the many metaphorical imprisonments he experiences throughout the book. Initially, he feels "imprisoned in High Rook House" (3) because of his weak heart and heavy debts, both of which enforce sobriety and limited activity. He fears the onset of nothingness and recalls an incident some years ago when, locked in a hotel lavatory, he came to realize he would prefer death to boredom. His constraints now force him to be satisfied with modest interests and distractions. He mocks the convention of prisons, but he nonetheless feels drawn to them and looks with amusement as a mouse, "a well known haunter of dungeons," (66) crawls across the floor. His best afternoon occurs when he and Maureen visit Len in Scratby Prison; his health and spirits improve directly as a result of his "imprisonment" in High Rook House; and his greatest success comes when he enters the Wallacian jail and retrieves Jane.

When Anthony is "released" from his financial confinement, he falls into a funk, drinking himself into the oblivion that is no longer enforced by his environment. Anthony feels exhausted from having to decide what to do with his life, lamenting that "fate had given him a second chance" and wishing "profoundly that he was where Len Winco-bank was, out of harm's way" (225, 246–47). Alison too begins to wish "she had not been presented with this sudden freedom of choice" (231). When they were constrained by sickening anxiety about their immediate future and so forced to limit themselves, they could manage the adversity. The freedom of committing sin, of backsliding, of once again sinking into depravity, is too great a burden. It isn't for Maureen Kirby, who enjoys her freedom and cheers Alison up with stories about her independence (237), but Maureen consistently presents an optimistic model, in direct contrast to the imprisoning suffering of the others.

Alison and Anthony share one peaceful night together, when they imagine themselves confined to "The smallest space, the smallest cell" (246). They will themselves into monastic seclusion.

> It seemed to them both that some secret was about to be revealed, was perhaps even there with them: the secret of living without ambition, agitation, hope. Intense silence flooded the house. They had stilled themselves to nothingness. It lasted: there it was. Neither moved, neither spoke. The fire faded. No sound from the world could reach them. Time paused: they heard its heart stop, they heard its breath hold, they heard the lapse of thudding and rustling and pumping and beating. They listened to the silence. (248)

This passage joins the image of Anthony's heart attack and the silence that had produced his earlier "aerial vision" to the metaphor of confinement. As in that vision, the cessation of activity, the imprisonment, serves as a test of faith and leads to revelation, for individuals, at least, if not for the entire nation.

But their moment of silence is shattered the next morning, and the second phase of Anthony's recovery begins and increasingly separates him from Alison. The difference in their responses to the crisis of Jane's imprisonment confirms the ambiguities of fate in the Providential model.

When Anthony receives Humphrey Clegg's call and subsequently travels to Wallacia to rescue Jane, he becomes marked for a destiny entirely different from Alison's. The technical reason why he goes instead of her is that her visa was issued by the previous Foreign Minister in Wallacia, who has subsequently been assassinated and whose authority is no longer recognized (252). She would not be able to renew her visa easily, and also Clegg feels more comfortable sending his secret documents with Anthony. Symbolically, however, Anthony is chosen because he can best respond to the destined confinement.

During her trip to Wallacia to visit her daughter, Alison feels caged, imprisoned in her hotel room, and she returns empty-handed. Indeed, she rejects Jane, emotionally and verbally, feels, with guilt, that she has cut herself free, and longs to escape. She neither rescues Jane nor establishes a new basis for their relationship, having no real comprehension of what prison means to her daughter. She does meditate in a local museum on the perversions created by "Gold. Money. Ambition" (112), evincing at least a potential for self-sacrifice, but she pulls away wanting "to turn back the clock, to six months ago, when all had been well" (113). Later, as she is preparing to return, she bitterly imagines herself as blinded Gloucester while chiding herself with Edgar's phrase, "What, in ill thoughts again?" (155). Instead of welcoming the opportunity to confront her culture's materialism, as Jane and Anthony in their different ways can do, Alison longs for the material comforts of England. Of course, Drabble also mocks Jane's foolish and naive alliance with the Wallacian communists, which is made in the name of revolt against her mother's, and England's, materialism. Jane remains childishly repugnant and selfishly obnoxious, sorely testing her mother's humanity and cultural openness by refusing to speak with her, even though she has come all this way to help her and has shown reasonable solicitude and constancy. Yet even so, we may feel Alison comes up short.

We may doubt that she would ever allow the revolutionary perspective in Wallacia to disrupt her fixed ideas.

Given that Alison believes misfortunes are caused by one's own thoughts or actions—a "primitive causality" she calls it (96)—we might speculate that if she had been caught by revolutionaries and imprisoned, she would probably have spent her time anxiously wondering what she had done to deserve her misfortune. Alison perverts the Providential model by believing that revelations of design will rigidly conform to her sense of guilt. She narrows her concept of fate to the dictates of her own will—"We choose what our own ill thoughts choose for us" (155)—so no external revelation can ever intervene. She feels damned no matter what she does.

Anthony too is tempted to see his heart attack as his own "choice," but he dismisses this view and considers it a warning, an accident that may lead to a new insight into Providence and that requires faith as a response. His spirits are slowly renewed and restored, especially through contact with Molly. She generates more feeling in him than anyone else because he can see her limitations as freedom. She even helps open him up to others; he takes her to the local pub and introduces her to a new friend, Ned Buckton, the warden of the local Youth Hostel (148). Ned is good with kids, and his example encourages Anthony to feel even more sympathy for Molly.

Alison cannot expand her personality when confronted with the limitations of Molly. Instead, she narrows her life, devoting all her attention to the cause of cerebral palsy and abandoning her husband, career, and elder daughter. Several times in the book she repeats what becomes her motto: "I can't split myself in two." She thinks that by confining all her energy into one cause, her own life will attain the completeness that she previously found in her beauty and in her acting career. But her devotion, more to the cause than to Molly herself, with whom she never feels comfortable, is too absolute and uncompromising. She has underestimated the demands of life, which entail being open to others, a model that is symbolized most by Jane's continual, chilling reminders of her abandonment.

After her trip to visit Jane, Alison expects to feel reunited with Anthony. But she feels resentment at his closeness to Molly. In contrast, Anthony feels sympathy for her, contemplating the beautiful mother, the handicapped daughter, and the resentful daughter, and he imagines the three forming "so eloquent a vision of irredeemable injustice and irredeemable pain" (182). Of course, he has had less to bear of Molly's problem, coming to it fairly late. But he is willing to ask, "What was it for? A joke, a trial, a punishment?" (182), while Alison sees it as an extension of her own will.

Anthony's questioning of fate continues to create new opportunities rather than morbid repetitions. When Clegg makes his proposal, Anthony thinks:

> He had been idly casting around for action, and here it was, it had presented itsef to him, it had picked him out. He could hardly refuse so mysterious a solicitation. (254)

Fate has come in mysterious form to Anthony, yet his response confirms the model that explains suffering as test of faith. The wheel of fortune turns again, but he sustains his openness to Providence. He resorts neither to superstition to externalize blame nor to neurosis to pity and to accuse himself. Rather, he accepts the "solicitation" of fate as a challenge for his growth.

He has as guides only a Le Carre novel, borrowed from Clegg, and a copy of *Antigone*, borrowed from Jane. Rejecting the incoherence of the design in the Le Carre novel and the random malice of the three fates in *Antigone*, Anthony demands a more rational response to the irrationality of fate. After a sequence of thriller-show adventures, Anthony finds himself in jail with a detective story, *Pickwick Papers*, and Boethius's *Consolation of Philosophy* to help him pass the time and justify the ways of God to man. He turns to Boethius, a fellow prisoner, exile, and, most important for Anthony, philosopher. Anthony tries to write a book in imitation of the Providential model Boethius supplies, and he manages some interest and faith in God, though he admits "his interest in God may be due solely to his peculiar situation" (294). He also admits his ineptitude as a writer, perhaps another of Drabble's self-parodies through which she acknowledges the inadequacy of her text yet implicitly claims by that acknowledgment a realism for her vision.

Boethius serves Drabble's purposes well, fulfilling the promise of the Miltonic epigraph and the implicit promise that the events throughout the book will be justified in the end by an appeal to an external order. Boethius stresses metaphors that have informed the development of *The Ice Age*: exile, imprisonment, disease, and the fickleness of Fortune. Anthony's finances and health make him a credible example of Boethius's contention that Fortune's gifts are transitory and hence not essentially owned by a person. Moreover, Anthony consistently strives for a perspective from which the multifold operations of chance will coalesce and create a simple pattern. He agrees with Boethius that the suffering of the righteous will conform to this pattern only if it is viewed as a test, a lesson in the ephemeral quality of earthly pleasure. On the one hand, this conclusion may be only an intellectual defense against the very real hardships and the terror he endures as a prisoner. On the other hand, this conclusion makes sense of his earlier uncertainties and discontents in a way that seems predestined for him to see.

Anthony "had been the victim of the most appalling bad luck, but he seemed to be taking it well" (293). We naturally want to know more about his faith in God and how well it actually works for him, but we are distanced from his renewal by the censorship of the Wallacian officials. He may be telling only what he thinks they want to hear, suppressing his discontent. However, he could be expressing his genuine, recovered faith.

James Gindin faults Drabble for creating the expectation that Anthony's fate will typify that of England, only to offer a recovery that seems typical of nothing more than a "commercially pedestrian fantasy" in the mode of "television adventure series."[3] But the completely unforeseen separation of Anthony from his friends and his family in England serves well to play off the Providential model. From this perspective, we need not think that Drabble intends for Anthony's vision adequately to fulfill the Miltonic vision of a "noble and puissant nation" rising once again. Drabble raises such a possibility, such an intertextual structure, in order to question it in the name of realism. Gindin doubts whether such intertextual play is in the name of realism, fearing that Drabble has only imperfect control over her irony as she creates a Miltonic resurrection in a far-away land. But the irony is secure; Anthony's vision is both more individualistic and more contingent than what the epigraphs call for.

The Providential model demands an explanation that clarifies and simplifies the vagaries of chance on a universal level. Anthony's imprisonment and philosophical speculation simplify only his own case. He serves a prison term for no crime he committed, yet this imprisonment leads him to greater self-understanding than the earlier "poetic justice" of his financial crisis. Censorship removes his insight from England—censorship both in realistic terms of the Wallacian government and in terms of the inexpressibility of Providence. The play with universal perspectives up to this point warns us against single explanations and demands a distance between the higher perspective of Providence and the mundane world of fate. Drabble forces us to see this distance:

3. James Gindin, "Three Recent British Novels and an American Response," *Michigan Quarterly Review* 17, 2 (1978): 233–35.

> This book too, like Anthony's, could have been about life in that camp. But one cannot enter the camp, with Anthony Keating. It is not for us, it is not, anyway, now, yet, for us. But we must acknowledge, we must pay our respects, within our limitations. Into some of Anthony's experience, we can enter. (295)

The intertext of the Providential model obtrudes here. Could a work of fiction embody Anthony's experience? Why cannot we have such an account? When would it ever be possible? Does Anthony really grasp a higher vision of order? Does life conform to it? Or is Anthony merely using a literary convention to constrain his experience? Drabble acknowledges this latter possibility when the narrator admits that Boethius's *Consolation of Philosophy* "influenced [Anthony] more than it should have done, perhaps, or would have done in other circumstances" (293). Drabble offers Anthony's vision as a possibility for someone, like him, who questions deeply and whom circumstance "favors" with a test of faith. But her novel deliberately, and justifiably, withdraws from defending that vision and applying it more generally. Providence remains an eternally receding vision, by definition ungraspable in mundane terms: it is an intertext that the realistic novel can respectfully acknowledge, but must set aside in the end.

Drabble herself expresses such a distance from a final vision. To Barbara Milton, just after finishing *The Ice Age*, Drabble said,

> I suppose we just never know what the pattern is. I suppose it is perfectly possible that one will die without knowing what it was all about. But I have this deep faith that it will all be revealed to me one day. One day I shall just see into the heart of the whole thing. A lot of people give up. They realize that there isn't an answer. Maybe that's what will happen to me. Maybe when I'm ten years older I'll decide that I was just deluding myself. But I haven't yet got to that stage.[4]

4. Barbara Milton, "Margaret Drabble: The Art of Fiction LXX," *Paris Review* 20, 74 (1978): 65.

The Ice Age tests the Providential model by positing, but then subverting, various external orders. All patterns and explanations for the random disasters and fortunes fail; all models of reality are deceptive. Characters never cease to find the challenges they are destined to find, but that destiny makes sense only in retrospect and only in individual cases. Anthony does not simply come to his vision arbitrarily, but rather he grows from his effort to comprehend the intertext dominating his situation. Nonetheless, his vision, insofar as it attempts to discern a universal design, may be seen as an arbitrary imposition of a formula onto an irredeemably quotidian reality. We are left hanging at the end, not knowing what to make of his revelation or of Drabble's intentions regarding the Providential model.

Alison, given the same or similar circumstances, withdraws. Her fate is to remain forever unchanged, and in this she may be more closely representative of England. Although this ending parallels Drabble's *The Realms of Gold* in its pairing of Frances Wingate, the optimist, and Stephen Ollerenshaw, the depressed suicide victim, *The Ice Age* presents an even more pointed vision of ordinary English life. Alison shares Stephen's narrow vision of life; however, the horror she represents is not a suicidally morbid mind but one drearily, hopelessly paralyzed by misfortune. Her life is beyond imagining because her own lack of imagination rigidifies and creates stagnation. True, the narrator tells us that Britain will recover, even though Alison will not, but we feel that the recovery indicated here is somewhat superficial and is probably limited to financial terms. Alison's self-destroying brittleness counters the open-ended possibilities of Anthony's vision. We cannot leave her because her state rests potentially in all who are crushed when they find their ideal mocked by others and by fate.

V. Conclusion

Fate may have outlived its usefulness as a doctrine of metaphysics; nonetheless, it still can indicate human attitudes and evoke conventional stories embodying those attitudes. Fate can suggest uncertainty about the future— "it's in the hands of fate"—though it implies that when the end comes, the outcome will seem in retrospect to have been inevitable. Fate can distance one from responsibility—"as fate would have it"—implying that an unforeseeable accident or unpredictable force is to blame for a turn in events. And fate can imply resignation to the influence of family and environment—"born to a fate of poverty and ill-use"—that predestines one's life, often unconsciously.

In our study, we have classified some specific attitudes and story structures often associated with the word *fate*: erotic, illicit passion in the tragic romance; attachment to home in the return to origin; and longing for justice in the Providential model. *Fate* implies that our lives are governed by such emotions, more than by reason or by knowledge. Schopenhauer, Emerson, and Nietzsche all translated Greek ideas about fate into conceptions of will in their philosophies of the irrational. *Fate* comprehends elemental truths of existence from which we cannot escape, yet which we can neither anticipate nor control.

Art formulates such truths and allows the reader vicariously to confront the irrational. By portraying overpowering emotions in stories with familiar contours, fiction teaches us to recognize inevitable consequences and to appreciate their form. But is recognition and appreciation enough? Realizing the intertextuality of fate implies a further problem, how to act in response to the inevitable. Should one passively accept it? Resist it? Or should one look for ways to live more comfortably with its decrees?

How can we avoid the Scylla of foolishly hoping to avert our fate and the Charybdis of weakly resigning ourselves to our lot, whatever that may be? How can one live in such a way that will invite grace, fate's alter ego, to bring unexpected relief from necessity? Will grace come from gaining consciousness of fate?

Drabble speaks frequently in interviews of being in harmony with fate, an acceptance of one's lot that invites grace.[1] Sometimes this acceptance comes from knowledge or, more properly, from wisdom: "The duty of the human will is to seek to make sense of [the world of chance] and to resist being swamped by the arbitrary and saying because it's arbitrary there's nothing you can do."[2] On other occasions, Drabble questions the efficacy of this struggle for wisdom, saying that we cannot change very much by our own endeavors.[3] In either case, knowledge is a fragile tool for molding character to accept fate and, by accepting it, to make fate less burdensome. Jane Gray, in *The Waterfall*, seeks determinedly to find a way of walking destined paths more willingly, but she fails despite her self-consciousness. How then might Drabble's stories make our fates easier to bear in such circumstances? Does knowledge of the intertext help in real-life situations?

Drabble considers the only moral or edifying purpose her fiction has is "to explore new territory. To extend one's knowledge of the world. And to illumine what one sees in it . . . to see better, clearer, more."[4] What will be the good

1. Nancy S. Hardin, "An Interview with Margaret Drabble," *Contemporary Literature* 14, 3 (1973): 284; Diana Cooper-Clark, "Margaret Drabble: Cautious Feminist," *Atlantic Monthly* (November 1980): 73; Joanne V. Creighton, "An Interview with Margaret Drabble," in *Margaret Drabble: Golden Realms*, edited by Dorey Schmidt. Living Author Series, no. 4 (Edinburg, Texas: Pan American University, 1982), p. 29.

2. Cooper-Clark, "Drabble," p. 73.

3. Barbara Milton, "Margaret Drabble: The Art of Fiction LXX," *Paris Review* 20, 74 (1978): 44; Hardin, "Drabbles's *The Millstone*, pp. 283, 289.

4. Milton, "Margaret Drabble," p. 59.

of this extended knowledge? Will wisdom drawn from novels teach us to accept our fate? Naturally, most of what we can say on this issue must derive from an analysis of Drabble's characters, but their testing of the bounds of knowledge teaches us that fate still can provide a means for identifying our true selves.

Early Drabble novels have characters who strive to avoid consequences of their actions, to delay or to outwit fate, even though they inevitably fail and are caught. Sarah Bennett, in *A Summer Bird-Cage*, announces a creed of fatalism, "I do believe that people can't be changed," but she follows this statement with "they can only be saved or enlightened or renewed, one by one." [5] She feels that knowledge can release her and her sister, Louise, from the tyranny of romance and family. Yet the knowledge she gains through the course of the book, from hearing about her sister's marriage and love affair, does not support a philosophy of renewal. Her own love life remains suspended in a fantasy of security all the while she listens to tales of degrading emotions. We suspect that when her fiancé, Francis, returns from America, Sarah will quickly find that her attempts to learn from the experience of her sister's marriage will have led to a fatal cynicism and doubt about love.

Emma Evans, in *The Garrick Year*, withdraws from her conflicts, hoping to defeat them by aesthetic detachment. She sees the consequences of a potential affair with Wyndham, but she maintains an aloof critical pose, inspecting and mocking him, rather than risk an embarrassing, crudely human involvement. But she gets trapped in the end by Wyndham's car as she tries to duck out of sight of her husband: a symbol of fate thwarting her attempts at escape and exposing her affair.

Rosamund, in *The Millstone*, is Drabble's first protagonist

5. Margaret Drabble, *A Summer Bird-Cage* (New York: William Morrow, 1964), p. 94.

who begins to understand and to accept her fate. The book begins by virtually parodying the tragic romance and the return to origin through Rosamund's dismissive treatment of George and her parents. But the complications of her pregnancy and motherhood make Rosamund question God's Providence: why was her daughter stricken with potentially fatal heart trouble? She has inherited from her parents a sincere concern for those who suffer, a sympathy that her pregnancy heightens and which deepens her understanding of the Hardy-like intertext she experiences. Her struggles have been a test of faith, and her adherence to motherhood gives her the reward of knowing herself, at least to some degree.

Jerusalem the Golden structures itself around models of fate: Clara's "fated" meetings with Clelia and Gabriel Denham (the tragic romance); Clara's attitudes toward her home town (the return to origin); and the telegram announcing her mother's illness, seemingly a fateful sign of retribution for her neglect (the Providential model). Clara grasps the implications of these models and elaborates their intertext by allusions to Hardy and other authors. Despite Clara's understanding, she remains rather selfishly fixated in a doomed quest for escape.

When Clara meets Clelia, the narrator tells us,

> she wondered . . . whether a conjunction so fateful and fruitful could have been, by some accidental obtuseness on her part, avoided: she did not like to think so, she liked to think that inevitability had had her in its grip, but at the same time she uneasily knew that it had, in some ways, been a near thing.[6]

Could she have missed this fateful conjunction? Her consciousness of the intertext of fateful meetings made her seize the opportunity, but this consciousness had only

6. Drabble, *Jerusalem the Golden* (London: Weidenfeld and Nicolson, 1967), p. 10. Hereinafter cited by page number in the text.

come to her recently, and if she had been less aware she might have missed her chance altogether. She overestimates her power and the significance of this meeting. The fate that she meets in Clelia and Gabriel in many ways only serves as a pretext for the more critical confrontation with her family, a fate she could never escape, no matter how uncritical she was. But she cannot see beyond the tragic romance of a first meeting and its selfish pleasures.

Clara, as a young girl, learns the intertext for a return home from *The Golden Windows*, a Sunday-school prize of her mother. The story treats a little boy who saw a house whose windows were all of gold. He searched for it and found to his disappointment that it was his own house with the sun reflecting in its windows (37–38). As Nora Stovel has explicated, this story comments ironically on Clara's attempts to belittle and reject her home.[7] And as Stovel points out, Drabble herself had a similar intertextual experience when she returned to Sheffield after writing *Jerusalem the Golden* and found the air cleaner than she remembered, making the city brighter and more like golden realms than the sooty industrial town she described in her novel.[8]

Clara never is able to apply the intertextual lesson she has learned. The telegram that informs her of her mother's cancer stuns Clara and challenges her understanding of fate. She had used her mother's illness (not knowing she was actually ill) as an excuse to leave school and go to Paris with her lover, Gabriel. Her guilt seems to prove that there is a moral justice, if somewhat vindictive, in the world:

> When Clara opened the telegram and saw the news about her mother, she trembled as though she had been struck from the heavens. She stood there, staring at the fatal yellow

7. Nora F. Stovel, "Margaret Drabble's Golden Vision," in *Margaret Drabble: Golden Realms*, pp. 4–9.

8. Drabble, *Arnold Bennett: A Biography* (London: Weidenfeld and Nicolson, 1974), p. 5.

paper, and her first thought was, I have killed my mother. By willing her death, I have killed her. By taking her name in vain, I have killed her. She thought, let them tell me no more that we are free, we cannot draw a breath without guilt, for my freedom she dies. And she felt closing in upon her, relentlessly, the hard and narrow clutch of retribution, those iron fingers which she had tried, so willfully, so desperately to elude; a whole system was after her, and she the final victim, the last sacrifice, the shuddering product merely of her past. (208)

Clara's thoughts circle around her growing recognition of a need for expiation for her foolhardy attempt to escape her fate, her mother, her ties to the past. She cannot escape her fate, yet she cannot see it in terms other than "sacrifice." When she does go home, her discovery of her mother's notebooks teaches her the need for compromising her freedom and expressing feelings of compassion for her mother's fate. But she represses the "golden windows" she discovers in her mother's notebooks when she cannot escape the dry, mockingly embittered tones of the past the next day when she visits her mother in the hospital (214–18). Her failure to apply the lesson of the return to origin highlights her lack of true self-awareness and growth despite the sophistication and the intelligence she showed in responding to the romance intertext.

As we have seen in *The Waterfall*, Jane Gray struggles at great length with the intertext of her fate, which she fully comprehends, but her knowledge brings little achievement or freedom. She seeks to escape her fate but finds that it catches her at each point; she can neither escape the tragic romance nor live with it in peace. Quite opposite is Rose, in *The Needle's Eye*, who comprehends little of the intertext she needs to live through but can allow what she does grasp to stimulate her self-knowledge and growth. Unfortunately, even the intertext cannot save her from the consequences of her fate, her permanent ties to the conflicts of her family. Unlike Clara, Rose accepts the consequences of these family ties in spite of their unpleasant aspect. We cannot say this wisdom brings transcendence because most of the time she feels bitterly embroiled in a marriage she may well wish had never been. But at times we see in moments of grace that Rose is blessed with a side to her character that ennobles simplicity and sincerity, which is in some ways the opposite of self-consciousness. She stands as Drabble's chief example of the good that can come from accepting fate.

The Realms of Gold presents a character who has both sophistication and simplicity, and consciousness of the intertext she lives out and acceptance of her limits. But Frances is less heroic than Rose in this regard because everything comes to her so easily. For Frances, fate is marvelously benign out of luck, not endeavor. The novel sets up a contrast between Frances and the depressives in her family, notably, Janet Bird and Stephen Ollerenshaw. Frances recognizes quite clearly the implications of her romance and return to origins, and in their ways Janet and Stephen also see the tie of fate quite clearly. But Frances is happy with her life and they are not. The difference is not a question of knowledge or of acceptance of fate, but of what their fates happen to be.

Frances is one for whom a "fatal messenger" brings news that her lover has been faithful to her.[9] Frances formulates the news according to the intertext of Greek tragedy, but she relishes with surprise the happy ending whose perfection suggests a poem or a play. Her consciousness of the intertext completes her self-awareness, making it more complex, but of course it cannot alter the outcome. We see her consciousness not as wisdom so much as the privilege of the blessed.

Similarly, her luck appears in many other references to twists of fate: The delayed postcard, her discoveries in Eel

9. Drabble, *The Realms of Gold* (New York: Knopf, 1976), p. 40.

Cottage of her great-aunt's love letters, her discovery of Tizouk. Even her lover's spouse decides to become a lesbian and exits the scene, allowing Frances to take over. When Frances visits her parents, she contemplates the potential suicidal danger in her inheritance of her father's moroseness and her mother's manipulative gaity. However, she finds the bonds of the past not asphyxiating but renewing. In a passage that recapitulates the return to origin, Frances acknowledges these bonds:

> One cannot escape one's destiny. And one day, in a moment of comic horror, it had occurred to her that in seeking to avoid her mother's ghost, she had in fact behaved exactly like her mother—she too had turned into a promiscuous and dominating flirt, the only difference being a technical one, in that she slept with the men instead of satisfying herself with verbal homage. But for Karel, she would have ended up like her mother. (81)

But of course there is Karel for Frances; she divorced her first husband and freed herself from the kind of conflict Rose endures with Christopher. Nothing better symbolizes Frances's lucky fate, her freedom, completed but not created by her recognition of the influence of her family.

When Frances's postcard telling Karel she loves him is delayed, she becomes excessively anxious and suspects rejection. The narrator scolds her and compares her reaction to *Tess of the d'Urbervilles* to illustrate the intertext of comic mishap, which Frances "should have been sensible enough to realize" (218). Like Tess, Frances allows her emotions to cloud her reason, but, unlike Tess, she has even more reason to be suspicious and to guess at the practical reason and the intertextual symbolism of the mishap. Frances cannot in this case see the intertext, yet she has the luck to get her man anyway. The intertext is irrelevant to her solving or coping with the problem, though it makes them laugh afterwards (351).

Janet and Stephen, despite their awareness of their

plights, reach immobilizing depths of pessimistic fatalism. They live out the ghastly family conditioning, the depression inherited from family and influenced by the landscape that Frances sees but keeps free from. Janet thinks bitterly about going up to bed with her husband, Mark, the caustic impotent, and refers to him as "my chosen fate" (174). Going to bed with him seems like disappearing into a volcano, the ruins of Pompeii, the melting of candle wax, a dead sea. David Ollerenshaw, the inert metal hunter, stares into a volcano—wittily sculpted by an intertextual self-mocking transition (176)—and Stephen Ollerenshaw broods on a "red-hot crater" in his parents' fireplace (188). They extend the volcano metaphor, making a symbol of the wider social pattern of depression Drabble depicts in this family history. But Stephen capitulates, he dives in, he is swallowed up by the intertext; he quotes Freud, Schopenhauer, T. S. Eliot, St. Augustine, and, of course, Empedocles on Etna. He knows the attractive, destructive force of fate. The narrator creates witty dialogue about and comment on the intertext, but for Stephen it is deadly serious and actually rationalizes his suicide. Stephen grows in Frances's mind to symbolize the victims of the world, including Karel's mother, killed by the Nazis: "it all seemed part of the same fate" (349). But his fate isn't part of the same fate, and Frances reveals her privileged position by not distinguishing between a suicide and the Holocaust.

How does one get Frances's privileged view? Most of us would choose her limited sympathies (which after all aren't that limited, as Stephen and Janet open up to her more than they do to anyone else), given her resilience, confidence, and self-awareness. Janet and Stephen, like many other Drabble characters, undercut themselves at every turn, allowing their marriages and other people's remarks to denigrate and destroy their lives. They blame fate, but is it because of fate that they are this way? Could they stop their self-destruction?

We might say that Frances is more "in tune" with her fate, that she accepts herself more, but what is this but to say again that she is lucky? Does she overcome serious defects in her personality? She does to some degree, given her background, but it comes easily for her. Is it her fate to overcome these defects? Or does she deserve our praise for not resigning herself to some depressive fate? Frances herself feels lucky not to be suicidal and calls it an accident that her younger sister committed suicide (52). When Frances and Janet talk together, Janet says she wishes she could look more sophisticated, as she did when they made her up to appear on TV: "Why could I never do that for myself?" (321). Why not? Is it a question of her fate or her free choice?

Drabble, in trying to reconcile character and fate, refers to the story of Oedipus and expresses her belief that in blaming fate one simply takes the circumstances and choices of one's life and externalizes them:

> I feel that the arbitrary is significant, but it's your fate to do the things that reveal the truth to you. Or perhaps it's your fate to see it later. I do believe in fate. I've had a peculiarly fated life, I sometimes think. But then if you look at it in another light, all that happens is that things happen to you and you're the kind of person that responds in a certain way.[10]

When our life assumes a recognizable form, we think we see the fate we have lived. But that fate may only be a way of tidying up what happens, a way of delimiting the mess of confused circumstances.

Mary Moran praises Drabble for expressing the traditional forms of the literature and the myths of our culture that shape the way we perceive our fates. She adroitly points out "one of Drabble's themes: the human need to give shape to raw experience by turning it into or seeing

10. Dee Preussner, "Talking with Margaret Drabble," *Modern Fiction Studies* 25, 4 (1979–1980): 567.

it in relation to a story."[11] But this shaping activity gains its virtue from the characters who employ it: morbid characters find morbid patterns, life-affirming ones find life-affirming patterns. Moran sees the role of vision and of literature in Drabble's works as continually affirming, whereas in fact vision and literature can only reflect the subjective motive of the person whom they affect.

When Kate, in *The Middle Ground*, listens to Ted narrate the story of Evelyn's accident, she thinks about the abortion she had and the strong pull she feels toward maternity.

> Fate had forced her to undo her own nature. I denied my nature, thought Kate, therefore nature cannot help me. Doing the right thing has destroyed me. What shall I seek, what help from the unnatural? Or must I simply admit the violence done, the death of a soul. (235)

Like Rose, Kate cannot resolve the dichotomy of fate and nature. Fate may seem external to her nature, but in the next sentence she admits she chose to act that way. What is fate but her choice? And what is her choice if not her nature? Motherhood was part of her nature, but so was her rational assessment that her plan was folly, that her desire to prolong her motherhood was an attempt to mask its passing. Kate, the journalist, knows the lives of countless women she has written about and can say what her feelings are because of this knowledge, but she cannot use the knowledge of the common patterns to save herself from a painful spiritual crisis. She chooses the intertext of a hostile and inhuman fate, a Hardy-like fate, to express her sorrow and self-doubt. It externalizes, it defines and delimits her life by admitting guilt. The recognition helps her to be her more optimistic self, but that self was what helped her to manipulate the intertext in that way.

11. Mary Hurley Moran, *Margaret Drabble: Existing Within Structures*, Crosscurrents Series (Carbondale: Southern Illinois University Press, 1983), pp. 113–114.

We find in *fate* a term to express our inexpressible feelings, as confused and cloudy and self-contradictory as they generally are when things go badly and we confront the unknown. *Fate* has a rich set of intertextual associations that come to the surface when we employ it. It cannot change fate to grasp it, for it is a term used in retrospect to identify a pattern in events that seemed confused when they occurred. Drabble compares life to a novel, saying, "As soon as the ending has occurred, then its inevitability is transparent to me. That's how it had to be . . . you have an illusion of making a choice or going in this direction or that, but when you get there you know there was no other way you could have gone." [12] But it serves the novelist's purpose in widening our range of perceptions. We see structures and formal arrangements where before we saw only the irrational behavior of humans and of nature.

As the widening scope of Drabble's fiction indicates, fate links the individual fate to the history of fates one knows from common lore and literature. One affirms one's humanity by uniting with all others who have felt the cold, inhuman blows of fate and who have expressed their anguish. Ironically, such intertextuality is itself as much a fate of the human condition as the experience expressed. We cannot suffer without speaking about it, and speaking about fate makes ourselves a part of a larger whole. Our attitudes toward those events we call fate will not change from our seeing this perspective, but they can and must be expressed. Like Anthony Keating, writing down his meditations in prison despite his consciousness of their clichéd nature, we can and must continue to describe patterns of fate in fiction and to pass these structures along to succeeding generations. They too will need words that give shape to destiny.

12. Preussner, "Talking," p. 566.

Selected Works by Margaret Drabble

Novels

A Summer Bird-Cage. New York: William Morrow, 1964.
The Garrick Year. London: Weidenfeld and Nicolson, 1964.
The Millstone. London: Weidenfeld and Nicolson, 1965. (Also published as *Thank You All Very Much*. New York: Signet, 1969.)
Jerusalem the Golden. London: Weidenfeld and Nicolson, 1967.
The Waterfall. London: Weidenfeld and Nicolson, 1969.
The Needle's Eye. New York: Knopf, 1972.
The Realms of Gold. New York: Knopf, 1976.
The Ice Age. New York: Knopf, 1977.
The Middle Ground. New York: Knopf, 1980.

Short Stories

"Hassan's Tower." In *Winters Tales*, vol. 12, edited by A. D. MacLean, pp. 41–59. New York: St. Martin's Press, 1966.
"A Voyage to Cythera." *Mademoiselle*, December 1967: 98–99, 148–50.
"Faithful Lovers." *Saturday Evening Post*, 6 April 1968: 62–65. (Also published as "The Reunion." In *Winters Tales*, vol. 14, edited by Kevin Crossley-Holland, pp. 149–68. New York: St. Martin's Press, 1968.)
"Crossing the Alps." In *Penguin Modern Stories*, vol. 3, edited by Judith Burnley. Harmondsworth, Middlesex: Penguin, 1969. (Reprinted in *Mademoiselle*, February 1971: 154–55, 193–98.)
"The Gifts of War." In *Winters Tales*, vol. 16, edited by A. D. MacLean, pp. 20–36. New York: St. Martin's Press, 1970.
"A Success Story." *Ms.*, December 1974: 52, 54–55, 94.
"A Day in the Life of a Public Woman." *Cosmopolitan*, 1973. (Also published as "A Day in the Life of a Smiling Woman." In *The Looking Glass: Twenty-One Modern Short Stories by Women*, edited by Nancy Dean and Myra Stark, pp. 143–65. New York: G. P. Putnam's Sons, 1977.)
"Homework." *Ontario Review*, Fall-Winter 1977–1978: 7–13.

Other Works

Wordsworth. Literature in Perspective Series. London: Evans Brothers, 1966.
Virginia Woolf: A Personal Debt. N.p.: Aloe Editions, 1973. (Also published as "How Not to Be Afraid of Virginia Woolf." *Ms.*, November 1972: 68, 70, 72, 121.)
Arnold Bennett: A Biography. London: Weidenfeld and Nicolson, 1974.
"The Author Comments." *Dutch Quarterly Review of Anglo-American Letters* 5 (1975): 35–38.
Editor, *The Genius of Thomas Hardy*. London: Weidenfeld and Nicolson, 1976.
A Writer's Britain: Landscape in Literature. New York: Knopf, 1979.